Wisdom for Aging Well

Wisdom for Aging Well

Richard A. Chancellor

iUniverse, Inc.
New York Lincoln Shanghai

Wisdom for Aging Well

iUniverse books may be ordered through booksellers or by contacting:

iUniverse
2021 Pine Lake Road, Suite 100
Lincoln, NE 68512
www.iuniverse.com
1-800-Authors (1-800-288-4677)

Because of the dynamic nature of the Internet, any Web addresses or links contained in this book may have changed since publication and may no longer be valid.

The views expressed in this work are solely those of the author and do not necessarily reflect the views of the publisher, and the publisher hereby disclaims any responsibility for them.

ISBN: 978-0-595-43692-7 (pbk)
ISBN: 978-0-595-88026-3 (ebk)

Printed in the United States of America

To Garner Senior Center
A home away from home

And

To my wife of over 50 years, Elizabeth and my
six wonderful grandchildren

David, Katya,
Eric, Leeza, Zoya, and Natya
In growth and development,
May God bless them.

Contents

Preface

Human life begins with a single cell and progresses through a series of developmental stages. It grows in early life and ages in later life. The final stage of human development, old age, can be the best or worst time of our life.

I have changed from a boy to an adult and to an eighty-year-old senior citizen myself. I have to revise my plan of life in ways that reflect both my goals and my values. What is prudent from the perspective of an early plan of life does not seem fitting anymore. I would like to share my personal experiences and feelings on the aging process with other elderly people. Maybe the sharing can benefit both of us.

This book is not a roadmap to golden aging. There are many ways to be happy in old age, just as there are many ways to be happy at any stage of life. One of the main purposes of this book is to help the readers and my fellow senior citizens develop perspectives for making sense of the process of aging.

The Chinese character on the cover of this book means "old" or "aging." I am a Chinese American, so I will describe my personal experiences and feelings from two cultural perspectives—East and West. This book begins by reviewing major demographic, historical, and cultural changes, facts and figures that will provide a resource for later discussion. I then turn to some accepted sociological theories about why we age, the aging process, the everyday life of the elderly, and the social programs available to them. The focus of this book is on health care, the fierce competition for public funds for human services, death and dying, and many other ethical issues closely related to senior citizens. I hope I can convince my fellow senior citizens that death is the final stage of growth in this fascinating process.

In the 2000 U.S. Census, the number of citizens sixty-five years and over in the United States was 35 million, 12.4 percent of our total population. This rate will increase in future years. It is projected that by the year 2030, the number of elderly will double, to approximately 65 million; at that time nearly one-fifth of the population will be sixty-five years old or older. Aging and unchecked spending of Social Security and Medicare are like a demographic tsunami that will never recede. No one knows how to solve this tough social problem. We should think about it, young or old, with an open mind, because we have no other choice.

Acknowledgments

It is a pleasure to thank those individuals and institutions who have helped me in the preparation of this book. I am especially grateful to Torrey Blackmar, director of Garner Senior Center, who helped me collect data and arranged interviews with some officials, such as Cheryl Gay, Garner Parks and Recreation Department, and Heather Burkhardt, Division of Aging and Adult Services. I also want to thank all the people working at Garner Center, whose services have made the center like a second home for all senior citizens.

Many great thinkers in the fields of sociology and philosophy have inspired me, either directly or indirectly, and I am very grateful to them. I also want to thank my son, Michael, and my daughter, Anna, and her husband, Kurt; they have spent time proofreading and making corrections and suggestions. A special thanks to my daughter-in-law, Dr. Ginny Dato, who suggested the title for this book. Another special thanks to my grand-daughter Katya for designing the book cover. Their efforts have made this book something I am very proud of.

1

Introduction

Demographic Changes

The United Nations states that to be classified as an "aged" society, a country must have a minimum of 7 percent of its population consisting of individuals aged sixty-five or older. According to the *CIA World Factbook*[1] on July 28, 2005, the ten countries with the most people aged sixty-five years and over were as follows:

Table 1.1 Countries with the highest percentage of citizens sixty-five and older (percentage)

Rank	Country	Percent
1	Monaco	22.4
2	Japan	19.5
3	Italy	19.4
4	Germany	18.9
5	Greece	18.8
6	Guernsey	17.8
7	Spain	17.6
8	Belgium	17.4
9	Sweden	17.4
10	Bulgaria	17.2
Weighted average of 227 countries		7.5

Source: *CIA World Factbook.* http://www.nationmaster.com, July 7, 2006.

1

The weighted average 7.5 percent is above the minimum 7 percent criterion set by the United Nations, which means that the whole world is an "aged" society. This is a serious social issue. For reference purposes, the percentages of aged populations of many other large countries are listed below.

Table 1.2 Demography of Senior Citizens

#12	Portugal	17.1
#17	Austria	16.6
#18	France	16.4
#23	Finland	15.9
#24	United Kingdom	15.8
#30	Hungary	15.1
#31	Denmark	15.0
#33	Norway	14.8
#38	Russia	14.2
#39	Netherlands	14.1
#43	Canada	13.2
#45	Poland	13.0
#46	Australia	12.9
#48	United States	12.4
#63	Argentina	10.6
#80	Chile	8.0
#86	China	7.6
#93	Turkey	6.7
#108	Brazil	6.0
#116	Indonesia	5.2
#128	Iran	4.9
#129	India	4.9
#138	Egypt	4.4
#142	Pakistan	4.1

There are few topics in this century that have more vast implications than aging. Today many countries have met the UN age criterion. We have lived longer and better than humankind has ever lived. In the nineteenth century few people lived long enough to retire; in the early twenty-first century those over seventy-five and eighty-five are the fastest growing groups in many countries.

Table 1.3 Population sixty-five years and over for the United States

Area	2000		1990		Percent change in 10 years
	Total population	Percentage of population over 65	Total population	Percentage of population over 65	
U.S.	281,421,906	12.4	248,709,872	12.6	12.0
Northeast	53,594,378	13.8	50,809,229	13.8	5.4
Midwest	64,392,776	12.6	59,668,632	13.0	6.6
South	100,236,820	12.4	85,445,930	12.6	16.0
West	63,197,932	11.0	52,786,082	11.0	19.9

Source: http://www.factfinder.census.gov, May 10, 2006.

Since 1900, the number of Americans sixty-five years and over increased from one in twenty-five, to one in eighteen by 1986, and to one in twelve in 2000 (2000 U.S. census).[2] This increase will continue in the future. It is projected that by the year 2030, the number of elderly will double, to approximately 65 million; at that time nearly one-fifth of the population will be sixty-five years or older.

Generational Equity

Never before have so many adults planned for an old age they will actually live to experience. The aging of society forces major changes in the institutions responsible for social well-being. The result is a heightened sense that the old and the young are in conflict. Especially, there is a growing perception that the old and the young are locked in fierce competition for a critical but scarce resource: public funds for human services, especially health care resources. The old and the young rally around a call for "generational equity."

It is primarily in this century that society has assumed direct responsibility for transferring certain goods and services from the young to the old. In human history, the responsibility for taking care of the old fell mainly upon families, as it still does for long-term care. There was no age-group conflict many decades ago;

taking care of the old was an individual or family issue and not a matter of social justice at all.

The aging of society has evoked a Malthusian forecast of doom: "The elderly produce little, yet their extensive needs give them large appetites for social resources. Government faces decisions about the allocation of public resources from a tax base that may experience slowed economic growth, but the growing numbers of the old make politicians eager to satisfy their appetite. However, shifting resources from the young to those needs will further undermine productivity, and so competition will occur under conditions of even greater scarcity."[3] What is a just and fair distribution of social resources among the different age groups competing for them?

Some blame the elderly for a great number of problems and costs that weaken America's ability to compete in the international economy. The distribution of resources between the young and the old is a serious conflict, and it will become even more severe in the near future.

The graying of America has increased the dependency ratio—the ratio of dependent (retired) persons to active wage earners in the population. This rising dependency ratio is causing difficulties for the Social Security system in particular, which could become bankrupt if the dependency ratio becomes too uneven.

According to the 2000 U.S. Census, the number of citizens sixty-five years and over in the United States was 35 million, 12.4 percent of our total population. On November 15, 2005 (as reported in *USA Today*), Mr. David Walker, the comptroller general of the United States, addressed a group of reporters on the unchecked spending of Social Security and Medicare and described it as a demographic tsunami that will never recede. He ran through a long list of fiscal challenges led by Medicare and Social Security benefits. No one knows how to solve these tough social problems.

My Personal Experience and Feelings

I am an eighty-year-old man. When I was young, taking care of aged parents was the family's responsibility. Today it is society's problem. I worry about the conflict over the distribution of resources between the young and the old, since the most rapidly growing age groups are those over seventy-five and eighty-five, the groups that need the most long-term care. There is no possibility of meeting future needs at today's growing levels without proportionally greater budgets for long-term care. It is thus likely that unmet needs will grow significantly. Can we afford continuing to spend up to 26 percent of the federal budget on benefits and services to an older population?

An aging population could place an unbearable burden on younger generations, with young workers being taxed heavily for pension funds. Or governments may have to cut back services for the young in order to fund services for the old. In a healthy, long-lived culture, many people will question the appropriateness of generous government support based on age, when there are so many people of all ages who are desperately needy. Without doubt, strains and serious fault lines are emerging in our dated intergenerational social programs.

To explain this conflict, Norman Denials says,

> If we treat the young one way and the old another, then over time, each person is treated both ways. The advantages (or disadvantages) of consistent differential treatment by age will equalize over time. A pattern of different treatment by race or sex at a moment will lead to different treatment over a lifetime, for these are fixed traits of individuals … therefore, problems of justice to be confronted. But a consistent pattern of differential treatment by age, over time, will erase the inequality it seems to entail, as long as that differential treatment is consistently administered. Differential treatment by age, over time, is not unequal treatment of persons, even if it is unequal treatment of age groups on each occasion, at each moment.[4]

I don't agree with this kind of justification. Justice is a function of time; people want justice now, not fifty years later. I don't think we can say to the young, "You should accept the unjust law now, because you will be treated differently fifty years from now." Time will not erase the inequality, only compensate it after it was done. For example, would you consider it just or unjust if your employer gives you your deserved pay raise fifty years later?

Of course this conflict will not happen tomorrow, nor will it even become a reality in my lifetime, but it will confront society before the twenty-first century is over. I write this book from a neutral stance, even though I am an eighty-year-old senior citizen myself. Aging is a serious matter in our life, and health care costs are a tremendous burden on our economy. We cannot avoid it; we had better face it. The following chapters will look at issues of aging both global and local, as well as my own personal journey through the aging process.

Notes

1. http://www.nationmaster.com, July 7, 2006.

2. http://www.factfinder.census.gov, May 10, 2006.

3. Norman Denials, *Am I My Parents' Keeper? An Essay on Justice Between the Young and the Old* (New York: Oxford University Press, 1988) 4, 10, 12.

4. Ibid. 41–42.

2

Aging in Human Experience

Why People Age

We begin to age as soon as we are born. A story says, "You don't grow old ... on purpose, the way you go downtown on a subway. It's more like finding yourself standing in the last station and wondering how you got there." In AD 8 the poet Ovid described this phenomenon very well:

Time in its stealthy gliding, cheats us all without our notice;
Nothing goes more swiftly than do the years.[1]

Aging is the deterioration of organisms that leads inevitably to their death. Human development is growth in early life and aging in later life. Why do we age and die? There is no simple answer. However, several theories have been proposed, and each of them says something important about the aging process.

The aging process is influenced by heredity, nutrition, health, and environmental factors, but we do not know exactly why people's bodies function less efficiently as they grow old. Human beings, like other species, have a maximum life span, a ceiling on the number of years that anyone lives. We have good reasons to believe that aging and death are genetically controlled. But how, exactly, do genes control aging? This is what is not yet known. None of the many theories of biological aging is universally accepted, but most of them take one of two basic approaches—"programmed aging" or "wear and tear."[2]

The programmed aging theory maintains that in each species, the body ages according to a normal developmental pattern built into every organism; each species has its own life expectancy and its own pattern of senescence—cells have an internal clock. Dr. Leonard Hayflick, a professor at the University of California, San Francisco, studied cells of many animals in laboratory, allowed them to divide or double, and measured the number of doublings that occurred. He found a limit on the number of times normal cells will divide. For example, a chicken's cells divide only fifteen to thirty-five times, while cells taken from

7

human embryos can double about fifty to sixty times—an estimate now referred to as the Hayflick limit.

It is not certain that Hayflick's limit applies to cells in living organisms the same way it applies to cells grown in laboratory. Still, there does seem to be some kind of genetic "aging clock" operating within cells that may, in interaction with environmental factors, cause cell death later in life. The limit controls the life span, which Hayflick holds as about 110 years for humans.

The wear-and-tear theory maintains that the body ages because of continuous use—that deterioration is the result of accumulated "insults." According to this theory, the human body is comparable to a machine whose parts eventually wear out.

One line of research supporting "wear-and-tear" focuses on the harmful effects of free radicals. Free radicals are unstable oxygen molecules that have only one electron instead of the usual pair and that try to latch on to other molecules. As they do this, they inflict damage on proteins, lipids, and DNA in the body's cells in a process known as oxidation. Think of an apple that has been cut open and left on the counter for a while. What happens to it? It turns brown. That is what oxidation does, and the same is happening inside our body.[3] Free radicals are specific forms of oxygen that are produced in the normal course of living but which then become highly dangerous, altering and damaging such substances in the body as DNA, proteins, and fats. This effect on cellular function has been associated with arthritis, muscular dystrophy, cataracts, and cancer. Thus, aging may result from the accumulation of irreversible destruction.

The difference between these two approaches is more than theoretical. If people are programmed to age, they can do little to retard the process, but if they age because of "insults" to the body, they may be able live longer by eliminating stressors. The truth probably lies in a combination of the approaches: genetic programming may limit the absolute length of life, but wear and tear may affect how closely a person approaches the limit.

Four Distinct Aging Processes

Aging is complex because of its many facets—physiological, emotional, cognitive, economic, and interpersonal—that influence our social functioning and well-being. It is a fascinating process because these changes occur differently in each one of us. Gerontologists view aging in terms of four distinct processes:[4]

1. **Chronological aging** is the definition of aging on the basis of a person's years from birth. Thus, a seventy-five-year-old is chronologically older

than a forty-five-year-old. Chronological age is not necessarily related to a person's physical health, mental abilities, or social status. It is only a legal identification.

2. **Biological aging** refers to the physical changes that reduce the efficiency of organ systems, such as posture, skin texture, hair color, strength, coordination, and sensory acuity. This is the functional deterioration of the individual's body, the real aging we cannot hide.

3. **Psychological aging** includes the changes that occur in sensory and perceptual processes, mental functioning, adaptive capacity, personality, drives, and motives. Thus, an individual who is intellectually active and adapts well to new situations can be considered psychologically young. Generally speaking, psychological aging is determined by one's feelings, attitudes, and manner of looking at things.

4. **Social aging** refers to an individual's changing roles and relationships in the social structure. As people age chronologically, biologically, and psychologically, their social roles and relationships also alter. The social context determines the meaning of aging for an individual. For example, our society has always tended to undervalue older people and to assume that most elderly are unintelligent, senile, and nonproductive. In my opinion, this one should have the least effect on our attitude.

We all age along these four dimensions—the chronological, biological, psychological, and social—although not necessarily at the same time or in the same way. The four interact and define our age norms. We cannot control chronological and biological aging at all, but psychological and social aging are the changes over which one has some control. For example, I feel as if I am biologically and psychologically younger than my chronological age.

Finally, although everyone who reaches old age faces a significant reduction in socioeconomic status, the economic well-being among the aged is not equal. Those aged individuals who have more resources than others may remain in closer contact with people and exhibit more activity. This can result in a higher self-concept, better adjustment, and less anxiety than others experience. In essence, the view the elderly have of themselves depends on factors of personality, health, sex, and socioeconomic status, but not necessarily at the same time or in the same way. I am absolutely sure that the aging process of Mr. Bill Gates will be quite different from mine.

Aging of the World

What was the experience of aging in prehistoric times? Hooyman and Kiyak describe it vividly in their book *Social Gerontology*.[5] They state that although our knowledge of the elderly in prehistoric and primitive societies is limited, we do know that people of advanced age were rare, with most dying before the age of thirty-five. During the hunting and gathering period in human history, the strength of our body was the means of survival; therefore, the elderly were then viewed as useless and were sometimes treated brutally. Those who outlived their usefulness were a heavy burden in societies. In some rural areas of ancient Japan, the elderly were carried into the mountains and left there to die.

In Greek and Roman cultures, 80 percent of the population perished before reaching the stage of life that we now consider middle age. In Medieval Europe, life expectancy was even shorter than in the Greek and Roman eras. The nobility lived longer than the common people during the Middle Ages, mostly because of a better standard of living. Furthermore, the general populace was more likely to die of war or the numerous diseases that plagued this era. Old age was depicted as ugly, weak, and deceptive.

In seventeenth- and eighteenth-century Colonial America, old age was treated with deference and respect, in part because it was so rare. The Puritans, for example, viewed old age as a sign of God's favor. Old men occupied the highest public offices, as well as positions of authority within the family, until they died; fathers waited until their sixties before giving their land to their eldest son. Church seats were given to the old. The primary basis of the power enjoyed by the elderly in colonial times was their control of property, especially productive property in farmland. In this agricultural society, such control amounted to the ability to dominate all key institutions—the family, the church, the economy, and the polity. Even though the old were exalted by law and custom in colonial times, they received little affection or love from younger people; in fact, most were kept at an emotional distance.

This pattern in Colonial America persisted until about 1770, when attitudes toward the elderly began to change. There are a number of indications of this change: church seating arrangements that had favored the old were abolished, the first mandatory retirement laws for legislators were passed, and the eldest son no longer automatically inherited the family property. A dramatic change was that parents began to live beyond the period of their children's dependency, and they became dependent upon their children.

In Asia, especially in agrarian China, the phenomenon of longer life expectancy was characterized by centrality of the family and reverence for the elderly. The respect was rooted in a tradition of ancestor worship and filial piety. The society was patrimonial and dependent on the land. The male was seen as a link in an unending chain of kin stretching back as far as ancestors could be traced, and forward into the future through his descendants. To break the chain by not having a male child was a failure to honor one's obligations to both past and future generations. Confucianism built on this premise of ancestor worship and provided a moral and intellectual foundation for revering the elderly.[6] Age in China, then, is considered an accumulation of wisdom, and people are proud of their age. Of course things are now gradually changing, because the growing pressures of limited housing and low income have a negative effect on younger generations' attitudes toward old people. But comparatively speaking, the elderly still enjoy more respect in the East than in the West.

The Effects of Modernization on Aging

Prior to 1930, the elderly enjoyed respect and held positions of leadership. In traditional societies, older people (usually male) exercised leadership and control. Until this century, an elderly person taking an afternoon walk could expect polite greeting from youngsters and could expect to be cared for by family members when health deteriorated.

The traditional status of the elderly has declined for many reasons: their increasing life expectancy and relatively larger numbers in society, urbanization and the geographical dispersion of the family, and social and upward mobility among young people. As early as 1893, Emile Durkheim, famous French sociologist, recognized the role of modern society in the decline in status among the elderly, remarking that the "worship of age is steadily weakening with civilization."[7]

The transformation of an entire society from a relatively rural way of life based on animal power toward a predominantly urban way of life based on inanimate sources of power, which emphasizes efficiency and progress, contributes to lower status of the elderly. As age becomes a less important criterion for determining access to and control of valued resources, the status and authority of society's elderly members tends to decline. Cowgill and Holmes identify the causes of this trend:[8]

1. **Health technology.** The application of health technology has reduced infant mortality and maternal deaths and prolonged adult life, thereby increasing the number of older persons in the population. With more

and older people in the labor market, competition for jobs between generations has intensified, and retirement has developed as a means of forcing older people out of the labor market.

2. **Scientific technology.** Scientific technology creates new jobs primarily for the young, with the elderly more likely to remain in traditional occupations that become obsolete. The rapid development of industries that rely on high technology in the twentieth century and the gap between generations in using computers illustrates this phenomenon.

3. **Urbanization.** In the early stages of modernization, when the society is relatively rural, young people are attracted to urban areas, whereas older parents and grandparents remain on the family farm or in rural communities. The resulting residential segregation of the generations has a dramatic impact on family interactions. The geographical and occupational mobility of the young leads to increased social distance between generations and to a reduced status of the aged.

4. **Literacy and mass education.** Modernization is characterized by efforts to promote literacy and education, which tend to be targeted toward the young. As young generations acquire more education than their parents, they begin to occupy higher status positions.

We can observe the trends described above in our own society: as the use of technology has increased, the elderly's control of important information and the esteem accorded them has declined. The elderly have experienced a reduction in leadership roles and influence.

While there is currently no official policy toward the aged, there is a very consistent and negative societal reaction to both the aged and the aging process. Instead of age being honored, obeyed, venerated, and serving as the basis for a hierarchically stratified society, the cult of youth has emerged and society has begun to loathe aging in others and fear it in itself (gerontophobia). Gradually, from 1910 up to the present, aging began to be viewed as a social problem.

America has become a youth-oriented society; the pervasive negative attitude (ageism) associated with gerontophobia is readily apparent. Thumbing through several of the more popular American magazines, such as *Time, Newsweek, Better Homes and Gardens, Good Housekeeping,* or the *Ladies' Home Journal* reveals numerous advertisements and articles focusing on how to stay young looking. The same attitude can be found in television or radio commercials broadcast daily, as well as in the books on the best-sellers list.[9]

In America, the aging process is viewed with anxiety and fear. An extensive negative stereotype of what it means to be old has developed. It is typified by following the ten myths:[9]

- Senility inevitably accompanies old age.
- The majority of old people are miserable.
- Most old people are lonely and isolated from their families.
- The majority of old people are in poor health.
- Old people are more likely than younger people to be victimized by crime.
- The majority of old people live in poverty.
- Older workers are less productive than younger ones.
- Old people who retire usually suffer a decline in health and early death.
- Most old people have no interest in, or capacity for, sexual relations.
- Most old people end up in nursing homes and other long-term care institutions.

According to most social gerontologists, it is this negative stereotype that begins to threaten individuals as they enter the middle stage of the life cycle. Once old age is reached, the aged are faced with both inevitable physiological decline and assignment to a lower social status. In sum, contemporary American society views the aged as less than useful, and it is not quite sure what to do with them.

There is a story that talks about the problem of the elderly in the modern world. It is funny but also very sad—it shows the negative attitude of the modern society toward old people.[10]

A ninety-year-old woman turns to her ninety-one-year-old husband and requests that he buy her some ice cream:
"Honey, I'd like some vanilla ice cream. Please write it down so you don't forget it."
"Don't worry, dear," is his reassuring response.
"Yes, but I'd like some hot fudge on it, some crushed nuts, a little whipped cream, and a cherry on top. But please, please write it down so you won't forget."
Husband: "I won't forget."
The spouse leaves and returns within the hour and hands his wife a salami sandwich.

She looks at it and angrily exclaims: "I told you to write it down—you forgot the mustard!"

Sociological Theories on How to Handle Aging

Aging causes various physical, psychological, and social changes. To cope with change, we must acknowledge that change has occurred. Denial is usually maladaptive. How do people adapt to these changes and achieve the generally positive adjustment that is the key to successful aging? To adjust to a change, we must first acknowledge that change has occurred. If a person denies that aging has affected personal performance when in fact it has, then it is difficult to adapt successfully. Adaptation is the process of adjusting to fit a situation or environment. The elderly have no choice but to adapt to less income, increased dependency, and lost roles or activities. Robert Atchley suggested three strategies that people can use in adapting to aging: *continuity*, *anticipation*, and *compensation*.[11]

Continuity is an important adaptive strategy that is available to most aging people. Many view continuity of lifestyle and residence as an important way to meet instrumental needs for clothing, food, shelter, and transportation. Continuity of independence and personal effectiveness is seen as a way to maintain self-esteem. Thus, for a wide variety of reasons, continuity is regarded as a central adaptive alternative in coping with many of the changes associated with aging.

Anticipation involves realizing beforehand what is likely to happen and taking action that can minimize or eliminate negative aspects and/or promote or increase positive aspects of changes. For example, we should estimate the financial resources needed to lead our desired lifestyle in retirement and take steps in advance for long-term care needs. Anticipation allows people to identify potential problems and find solutions before problems actually develop.

Compensation involves taking actions that offset or make up for a loss in function. Eyeglasses and hearing aids are the most common examples of compensations for physical age changes. Compensation can sometimes restore a person to the same level of capacity she or he enjoyed before a change occurred, but more often compensations are imperfect; therefore, compensation itself often requires adaptation.

Continuity, anticipation, and compensation are general strategies for coping not only with the change of aging but with all changes. The patterns of adaptation that people follow vary with personality and life circumstances. A person sitting in a rocking chair on the front porch is no less healthy than a person busy all day long. What is the proper way for old adults to adapt? There are a variety of theoretical approaches addressing how people should adapt to aging:[12]

1. **Disengagement theory.** For too many years, it was believed that the best way to age was to be disengaged. Disengagement theory argues that as older adults slow down, they gradually and voluntarily withdraw from society, while society encourages this by pressuring people to retire. Reduction of social interaction and increased self-preoccupation was thought to increase life satisfaction among older adults. This decline in social interaction theoretically helps older people to keep their balance and benefits both the individual and society. Disengagement theory claims that successful aging involves a mutual withdrawal of the aging individual and society.

2. **Activity theory.** This theory holds that the more active older people remain, the better they age. Activity theory suggests that people should continue their middle adulthood roles through late adulthood, keep up as many activities as possible, and find substitutes for activities lost through retirement—for example, by replacing work with golf, volunteer work, or other stimulating pursuits. In this view, a person's roles (worker, spouse, parent, and so on) are the major source of satisfaction in life; the greater the loss of roles through retirement, widowhood, distance from children, infirmity, or other causes, the less satisfied the person will be.

3. **Role theory.** This theory suggests that when people age, they must adjust to a variety of conditions that were not part of their previous social roles. These adjustments generally fall into two major categories: relinquishing social roles and relationships typifying adulthood, and accepting social roles and relationships typifying old age, such as giving up an independent place of residence, reducing interest in planning for distant goals, increasing dependency on others, and subordinating to one's own children.

4. **Subcultural theory.** The theory parallels role theory and disengagement approaches. A subculture emerges when a group of people interact with each other more than they do with others for either of two reasons: as a result of a positive affinity with each other or because all members of one group are excluded from interacting with members of other groups. This theory suggests that the behavior of the

aged be viewed and analyzed from the perspective of their participation in the aged subculture, just as we would analyze other social problems, such as juvenile delinquency.

5. **Age-stratification theory.** This theory may be equated to an aggregate-level version of role theory. Each stratum represents a different social role to be learned by those who enter it, played by those who remain in it, and given up by those who leave it. This theory suggests that the aging process be analyzed by a class theory based not on socioeconomic status but on age status. In other words, the aging phenomenon may best be understood by examining the stratification of the age classes.

While the five major approaches emphasize different aspects of the aging process, they all focus around one factor, the changing social role of the aging individual. Regardless of which theoretical approach one takes, there are two main issues to consider: how society views the aged and how the aged view themselves. No matter which approach one adopts, the change must be spiritually and intellectually enjoyable for each individual. Different approaches can add different difficulties in social life.

We have seen evidence that individuals who remain active in old age benefit from their activity. Those who are physically active retain their health longer than those who lead sedentary lives. Those who are intellectually active are likely to maintain their cognitive functions longer. In other words, there seems to be more support for activity theory than for disengagement theory. Dr. John Brantner, a clinical psychologist and professor, suggests four activity principles for good adjustment to growing older:[13]

1. **Be open.** This means that we need to find someone—our spouse, a friend, or a counselor—we trust and with whom we can share our distress.

2. **Be lighthearted.** Celebrate life and death. Avoid despair, depression, and hopelessness.

3. **Keep active in every way.** Keep active mentally, physically, emotionally, and spiritually: "I will wear out and not rust out."

4. **Reach out to others.** Behave in an extroverted way, remaining sociable and adding acquaintances at every opportunity.

Richard Aldington makes a few more suggestions that can help us experience the true adventure of active living:[13]

- Renew energy! (Recognize enthusiasm as a source of energy.)
- Resist laziness! (We cannot sit on the rocking chair waiting for death.)
- Avoid procrastination! (Procrastination is the thief of time.)
- Banish boredom! (Boredom and laziness are intertwined together.)
- Seek balance! (Stretch the body, the mind and the self!)
- Explore new ideas!
- Dream dreams!
- Set goals!
- Take action!

By contrast, a man who earlier in life found work to be a hassle might like better in his retirement years to take it easy, do a little fishing, and sit on the porch; he might be extremely unhappy if he were forced to continue working. In fact, older people are likely to be most satisfied when their retirement lifestyles suit their individual personalities and preferences. General recommendations from the medical field about how to handle aging include the four following commonsense rules, which people of all ages can use to improve their health:

- Stimulate the brain.
- Improve physical fitness.
- Have a balanced diet.
- Manage stress.

So far, research has not shown that either of these two theories (activity theory and disengagement theory) is more accurate than the other. Neither one of the five theories adequately allows for individual differences in personality traits and preferences. Each person is different; we cannot assume what suits one suits all. Rather, we should adopt an interaction model of development that emphasizes the goodness of fit between person and environment.

Sociological theories suggest that rather than a single pattern of optimum aging, what we see is a diversity of patterns of aging based on combinations of personality type, role activity, and life satisfaction. Another phenomenon is the difference between men and women. Older men face more acute health problems and a shorter life expectancy than women. Many married women will spend the last twenty years of their life without a spouse. Widowhood represents a serious social problem, and it can lead to ongoing loneliness and depression.

In addition, we have to face the cold fact of economic status. Although everyone who reaches old age faces a significant reduction in socioeconomic status, economic well-being among the aged is not equal. Income differences among people are an obvious factor in varied experiences of aging. Middle- and upper-class individuals are much more likely to enter retirement with assets and private pension funds, along with their Social Security benefits. In addition, income often interacts with occupational status to affect aging. For example, men from lower socioeconomic classes leave school earlier and begin working earlier, generally in blue-collar or service jobs. These men may retire sooner and thus see themselves as being old at younger ages than do middle-class men.[14] In essence, how the aged view themselves depends on factors of personality, health, sex, and socioeconomic status. Money is still one of the factors that affect the quality of our aging.

My Personal Experience and Feelings

As I am aging, I have changed role from father to grandfather. After retiring, I changed roles from mechanical engineer to lifelong student of social science. I stopped going to Quality Engineer Club and instead joined the Garner Senior Center. My activity concentrates on school instead of on my job. All these changes indicate that I have adopted role theory, subcultural theory, and age-stratification theory approaches in my aging process. I have done so either subconsciously or consciously, but with no choice other than to follow them automatically, according to my aged subculture and age status, like water running from high to low.

The only theories of these five about which we have some choice are activity theory and disengagement theory. I feel the five theories, especially the activity theory and disengagement theory, are too extreme; our life is not restrained and does not have to follow any single approach for us to be happy. I prefer Aristotle's Doctrine of the Mean.[15] Originally the Doctrine of the Mean was concerned with feelings and actions, in which excess and deficiency are in error and incur blame, while the intermediate condition is correct and wins praise. Successful aging involves choice, and the correct choice is the mean.

This Doctrine of the Mean emphasizes that when we express emotions and do things, we take a balance of two extremes. In the aging process, we disengage in some areas and engage in the other; we become active in some fields and inactive in the others. For example, we disengage from work but we are still engaged with our family and society; we may be active in exercises but maybe not in art. I like table tennis but not basketball. Successful aging is a balance between our personality and circumstances no matter what strategy we use.

As a habit, I take a walk every morning. One day I found lots of worms crossing the road from one side to another. Many of them were run over by cars or human steps and pressed to a black line on the road surface. I tried to pick up some and help them cross the road before the accident happened. But there were so many, I just could not help them all to make this journey. I had great sympathy for them, so I wrote a poem, "Many Worms Cross the Road," to express my sorrow—and also to express my personal view about life. The phenomenon of "many worms crossing the road" is an analogical example of the Doctrine of the Mean—crossing the road from one side to another is too extreme for a worm.

Many worms cross the road
From one side to another.
It is too far away for you
To make it!

❧

Many things can happen:
Tire may run over you,
Foot may step on you,
And leave a black line on the road surface.
Your life must be worth
More than
A line?

❧

Why do you want to cross the road?
From one side to another
Is not like
From Hell to Heaven;
There is not much
Difference.

The Doctrine of Mean can be used in all fields of our life: extremes may bring instant excitement, but it is the mean that holds harmony and long-lasting happiness. Living with basic essentials and receiving pleasure out of nonmaterial experiences is better than satisfying our needs by constantly seeking more goods and services—this attitude is the practice of the Doctrine of Mean. No matter which one of the five theories of aging you adopt, practicing the Doctrine of Mean will bring you successful old age.

Notes

1. Susan H. McFadden and Robert C. Atchley, eds., *Aging and the Meaning of Time* (New York: Springer Publishing Company, 2001).

2. D. E. Papalia and S. W. and Olds, *Human Development*, 6th ed. (New York: McGraw-Hill, Inc., 1995), 533.

3. Reader's Digest, *Looking after Your Body: An Owner's Guide to Successful Aging* (New York: The Reader's Digestion Association, Inc., 2001) 18–19.

4. R. Nancy Hooyman and H. Asuman Kiyak, *Social Gerontology*, 3rd ed (Boston: Allyn and Bacon, 1993), 2.

5. Ibid. 54–55.

6. Laura Katz Olson, *The Graying of the World: Who Will Care for the Frail Elderly?* (New York: The Haworth Press, 1994), 262–63.

7. Fermando M Torres-Gil, *The New Aging, Politics and Change in America* (London: Auburn House, 1992), 9–10.

8. Hooyman and Kiyak, *Social Gerontology*, 55.

9. Fredric D. Wolinsky, *The Sociology of Health* (Belmont, CA: Wadsworth Publishing Company, 1988), 178–79.

10. U. A. Falk and G. Falk, *Ageism, the Aged and Aging in America* (Springfield, IL: Charles C Thomas Publisher, Ltd., 1997), 179.

11. Robert C. Atchley, *Social Forces and Aging* (Belmont, CA: Wadsworth Publishing Company, 1994), 361–65.

12. Wolinsky, *Sociology of Health*, 175–78.

13. Gari Lesnoff-Caravaglia, *Values, Ethics, and Aging* (New York: Human Sciences Press, Inc., 1985), 154–55, 200.

14. Philip R. Popple and Leslie Leighninger, *Social Work, Social Welfare, and American Society*, 4th ed. (Boston: Allyn and Bacon, 1999), 566–67.

15. Cohen, Curd, and Reeve, eds. *Ancient Greek Philosophy* (Indianapolis: Hackett Publishing Company, Wadsworth Publishing Company, 1994, 1995), 679.

3

Everyday Life of the Elderly and Living Arrangement

Meeting the Needs of Older Bodies

Societies generally distinguish between three classes of elderly:[1] those who are no longer fully productive economically but are physically and mentally able to attend to their daily needs, those who are totally dependent and require custodial care, and those who continue to participate actively in the economy of the social system. I will concentrate first on the everyday lives of the healthy ones in this chapter.

I think all adults have the similar feeling that when they were young, the physical environment was just too big for them: the chair and table were too high and the stairways were too steep. The physical environment of society is mainly designed for adults, not for children, and not for the elderly either. The physical changes of aging cause thousands of mismatches in the way we interact with the world around us, changes so subtle that we often don't notice them at first. The everyday lives of the elderly, in terms of the environment, are not the same as those when they were younger and healthier.

In an attempt to determine how the standard physical environment becomes less form fitting to an old person, the Gallup Organization asked 1,500 non-institutionalized people fifty-five and over in 1990 what they might need help doing in order to stay self-sufficient and feel comfortable in their environments. When asked what they considered to be the main problems of everyday life, those surveyed identified the following sixteen areas:[1]

1. Opening medicine packages

2. Reading product labels

3. Reaching high things

4. Fastening buttons, snaps, or zippers

5. Vacuuming and dusting

6. Going up and down stairs

7. Cleaning bathtubs and sinks

8. Washing and waxing floors

9. Putting on clothes over one's head

10. Putting on socks, shoes, or stockings

11. Carrying purchases home

12. Using tools

13. Being helpless if something happened at home, since no one would know

14. Using the shower or bathtub

15. Tying shoelaces, bows, and neckties

16. Moving around the house without slipping or falling

What these problems have in common is that they are minor inconveniences that can rapidly make life impossible as we age, as our mobility is reduced, or our senses are impaired. I would like to add some things that I feel are difficult to cope with:

- It is difficult to cut my toe nails, because I have a hard time reaching and often cut my toe skin due to the stiffness of my hands.

- It is difficult to pick up things that have fallen on the floor because of knee arthritis.

- I have difficulty understanding the message on the telephone answering machine because the message is not clear or too fast, or voice is too low.

- Handwriting is hard because of shaking hands.

- Cooking is too much a burden in everyday life, so I don't eat properly.

- I lock myself out of the car often.

- It is difficult to lower windows in winter and raise windows in summer.

- I misunderstand others or miss appointments because of partial hearing loss.

- It is difficult to adjust the timing on clocks and watches due to loss of dexterity in my fingers.

- Entering and leaving the car requires special effort because of knee arthritis and backache.

- I am afraid to drive in the evening because I cannot see the signs well enough from a distance to make a decision on time.

- It is difficult to back up a car and parallel park because I cannot turn my neck as far as I would like to.

- Non-stop dreaming and getting up too often at night deteriorate the quality of my sleep, which, as a consequence, affects my daytime activity.

Hence, the support the old people seek from their families and society will be not only financial but also emotional and social. The question that remains yet to be answered is, "Can the American family accommodate its own old people?" Will anyone speak to Grandma, or will everyone ignore her and talk around her, away from her, and "over her head"? What needs to be explored is how families can alleviate the pain of the old, who are treated everywhere as if they had no body and no soul and, above all, no ability to make their own decisions. Years ago, Shel Silverstein put it best when he wrote this poem:[2]

> Said the little boy: "Sometimes I drop my spoon,"
> Said the little old man, "I do that, too."
> The little boy whispered "I wet my pants,"
> "I do that too," laughed the little old man.
> Said the little boy, "I often cry,"
> The little old man nodded, "so do I."
> "But worst of all," said the boy, "it seems, grown-ups don't pay attention to me."
> And he felt the warmth of a wrinkled old hand, "I know what you mean," said the little old man.

No doubt, the most painful experience for the old in American society is the status change we must undergo when we are relegated to the position of a nonperson. A nonperson is here defined as someone who is indeed alive but receives no recognition in the most ordinary meaning of that word. Social recognition is, of course, the very content of life.

Living Arrangements

"How to live" is a financial and emotional decision, which is a value judgment. Each person's choice is different, especially for the elderly. No single approach that fits one will fit all.

Most seniors prefer to live in their own home in a familiar environment, but if they cannot drive anymore, or are unable to maintain a home, or are tired of cooking, "independent living" is worth consideration. Independent living provides many conveniences while respecting tenants' desire for privacy. I visited quite a few independent living facilities in the Raleigh area, and I have included here the following list of services, as well as pricing:

- Three meals a day, seven days a week

- Transportation services

- Housekeeping services

- Escort/errand services

- Exercise and wellness programs

- Educational programs, outings, and events daily

- Staff available around the clock in case of emergency

- Access to on-site wellness center

- Access to on-site banking and postal services

- Extra charge for supportive living

- Studio with one bath is about $1500 to $2000 per month, and $500 more for second occupant

When I asked seniors what they fear most about aging in terms of living arrangement, the general response from the elderly is that people fear the inability to anticipate what the future might bring and the process of dying, particularly the prospect of dying slowly and in pain. They just don't know how to cope with it.

Our life's course is characterized by varying periods of greater or lesser dependency upon social relationships. Generally speaking, those who are totally dependent require custodial care; they do not have much choice. (The next chapter will discuss social programs.) In both the West and the East, the elderly have used their rights over property to guarantee their security by compelling others to support them or to provide them with goods and services. The traditional extended household is an example. Elders in wealthy households enjoy higher status within the family and are better able to control the lives of their adult children than those in poor households. As economic resources decline and class differences disappear in these cultures with increasing modernization, the traditional filial piety has become undermined.

The control of property is a means of achieving power in most societies. Both in past and present times, the elderly have used their rights over property to guarantee their security by compelling others to support them or to provide them with goods and services. Control over knowledge, especially ritual and religious knowledge, is another source of power. A basic principle governing the status of the elderly appears to be the effort to achieve a balance between older people's contributions to the society and the costs of supporting them.[3] Corin outlines four ways in which a person can cope with a life event or change in lifestyle that requires assistance:[4]

- A reliance on one's own resources

- The use of informal resources

- The use of formal resources

- A mix of one's own resources and informal and formal resourses

Control of resources as a basis for social interactions between members of a society is important throughout the life cycle. However, it becomes even more crucial in old age, because retirement generally results in a decline in one's level of control over material and social resources. Both in past and present times, the family can play an important role in supporting the old.

Of the total population of older Americans, 43 percent are single. Already, 10 percent of today's senior citizens have children who are also senior citizens. Learning to lovingly care for our older family members and friends without overwhelming ourselves will become a challenge in the family. The average American woman can expect to spend more years caring for her parents than she did caring for her children.

Besides the traditional family, Ken Dychtwald, in his book *Age Wave*, reinvented the family to include the elderly; he calls it "matrix family."[5] This matrix family is uniquely matched to the characteristics of the age wave. It is not the nuclear family with parents and children, but a relationship between adults bound together by friendship and choice as well as by obligation. This family can have more than two adults or a group of people; they form a matrix to take care of and be companions to each other.

Many single senior citizens have already created such a "matrix," and more may give this idea a favorable consideration. Maybe you will be able to find compatible people to form a matrix family to help one another. Of course, it is not easy to find like-minded friends, but you should not stop looking. Who knows what will happen tomorrow? This idea of matrix family may benefit you as an individual and also reduce the burden on your children and society.

My Personal Experience and Feelings

"How to live" is a personal decision. Since antiquity until today, philosophers have studied two main questions: (1) what truth is, and (2) how to live. Neither is easy to answer.

One year after retiring from my engineering career of forty years, I registered at North Carolina State University in January 1996 as a full-time student majoring in philosophy. In my entire life, I had learned only the skill I needed to make a living and support my family; I really don't know much about humanity and society. Retiring from active work and freed from pressure, I have time to think about what I want and how to live. I have a burning desire to know "What is the meaning of life?" before it's too late. That is the reason I chose philosophy as my undergraduate study and sociology as my graduate study. Studying is not only my life but also a means to seek the truth. Studying brings me lots of happiness, which I cannot get any other way. I am going to live life as a student for the rest of my old age (or until I become senile).

As I mentioned above, my intention is to find the meaning of life before it is too late, but this brings me some trouble. At the end of each semester, my grandchildren always ask me, "Grandpa, have you found the meaning of life yet?" and I say, "I am sorry, my dear. Not yet." They keep asking me the same question, "Have you found the meaning of life yet?" semester after semester, and I feel very embarrassed to give them the same answer, "Not yet," year after year.

Every human being should answer the question of "how to live" seriously. Life is not just killing time. I don't think that only great people can have a life with meaning. If we are living beings, there must be a meaning, one that is innate from birth. There are many things in the world we can do in our life, and each one is different, but there are two things in common to all living beings on earth: we all "work and learn!"

Whether you like it or not, and no matter who you are, you cannot be born to this world without doing anything; such a life is meaningless and impossible. Doing something is work; trying to do it better next time, consciously or subconsciously, is learning.

That is not all. Not only human beings have to work and learn; even animals have to work and learn. They have to find food, look for a mate, and avoid danger. They have to learn how to do these things better day after day to survive. Therefore, my conclusion is that, in realistic sense, the meanings of life is this: "work and learn." The very words contain happiness in themselves. I will tell my grandchildren about my finding, and I hope they will stop asking me, "Grandpa, have you found the meaning of life yet?"

I am so absorbed in my study and so busy making friends with the great thinkers in books that I even don't feel any need of the outside material world to be happy. I live a serene life in a busy and noisy world. I have made a will with a list of my favorite books, and I will tell my son and daughter that these books must be buried with me. I may need them for reference.

Today, continuing education during adulthood is necessary because of rapid technological and social change. Learning has also become a leisure pursuit in which an individual can learn for the sake of learning regardless of chronological age or stage in life. With increasing opportunities to pursue educational programs, a growing percentage of the elderly population is enrolling in educational courses as a form of leisure in their pre- and postretirement years.

Furthermore, it is recognized that continued learning and problem solving in later life can sustain and even improve intellectual abilities, attitudes, interests, and longevity. The stimulation provided by an educational atmosphere is an enriching experience for many elderly people, and it is thereby important to their physical and mental health.[6]

Aging is just the last stage of life. My attitude in adapting to aging is to treat it the same as my early adult life. The only difference is that I don't have to work to make a living anymore. In my mind, I consider myself a traveler on a long journey, starting early in the morning and walking steadily toward the beautiful sunset.

Notes

1. Ken Dychtwald and Flower Joe, *Age Wave* (New York: Bantam Books, 1990), 312–13.

2. U. A. Falk and G. Falk, *Ageism, the Aged and Aging in America* (Springfield, IL: Charles C Thomas Publisher, Ltd., 1997), 93.

3. Nancy R. Hooyman and H. Asuman Kiyak, *Social Gerontology*, 3rd ed. (Boston: Allyn and Bacon, 1993), 59.

4. Barry D. McPherson, *Aging as a Social Process* (Toronto: Harcount Brace & Company, 1998), 319.

5. Ken Dychtwald and Flower Joe, *Age Wave* (New York: Bantam Books, 1990), 236–37.

6. Lewis R. Alken, *Later Life*, 2nd ed. (New York: Holt, Rinehart and Winston, 1982), 90.

4

Social Programs and Services for the Elderly

General Description around the World

In her book, *The Graying of the World: Who Will Care for the Frail Elderly?* Laura Katz Olson mentions that every country, regardless of its political economy, is struggling with various political, social, economic, and psychological issues associated with caring for growing frail populations.[1]

In Sweden, Finland, Israel, and France, the public sector is responsible for its dependent older population. Neither the individual nor the family is expected to shoulder the entire burden of care. Health care and social services in these countries are presumed to be "rights." The dominant view is that the aged are entitled to receive all types of care. Despite the growth of supportive services, the family still plays the dominant role in the actual care of chronically ill spouses and parents.

In Britain and Canada, the state plays a relatively minor role in the direct provision of long-term care. The family is the preferred caregiver; and programs are developed only to fill gaps when kin are not available.

In Japan, over 60 percent of people aged sixty-five and over, and nearly 80 percent of those aged eighty and over, live with their adult children; fewer than 10 percent live alone. The dependency of older people in the family is culturally sanctioned. Familism, based on the Confucian concept of filial piety, promotes mutual support, cooperation, and obligation among the generations. By comparison, there is a high proportion of people without adequate support in rural areas than in urban areas.

Similar problems exist in China, where few state programs or policies are directed at the rural elderly. Frail older people in the People's Republic of China are a low priority in the allocation of public resources. State social welfare policies for the chronically-ill aged tend to reinforce the role of the family. The institutional facilities in China are available mainly to the childless and ambulatory population. Both in Japan and China, where Confucianism mandates male filial responsibility for aging parents, it is the daughter-in-law who provides the actual care.

The United States has not developed a comprehensive national policy for universal long-term care. The issues and problems of old age are viewed as private problems requiring private solutions. American policies presuppose that individuals and their families should and will provide for their own social, financial, and service needs. Eligibility for publicly subsidized support, which mostly funds institutional care, is based on personal insolvency. This combination of a reliance on individual resources and a welfare approach to caregiving has generated a two-class system of elder care. The trend toward privatization of hospitals, nursing homes, sheltered housing, and home care will enlarge the gap between the "haves" and the "have-nots" among the aged.[2] Health care must be provided in such a way as to show the elderly that we value them as human beings. A profit-making environment is unsuitable for the development of such facilities. In the absence of a comprehensive and affordable health care system for younger generations, the vast majority of Americans entering middle and old age will be vulnerable.

Social Programs in the United States

All people through human history have faced the uncertainties brought on by death, disability, and old age. Prior to the turn of the twentieth century, the majority of people in the United States lived and worked on farms, and economic security was provided by the extended family. However, this arrangement changed as America underwent the Industrial Revolution. The extended family and the family farm as sources of economic security became less common. Then, the Great Depression triggered a crisis in the nation's economic life. It was against this backdrop that the Social Security Act emerged.[3]

Federal legislation to promote economic security was recommended in President Franklin D. Roosevelt's Message to Congress on June 8, 1934. The Social Security Act became law with President Roosevelt's signature on August 14, 1935. As President Roosevelt said at the ceremony:

> The civilization of the past hundred years, with its startling industrial changes, has tended more and more to make life insecure.... We can never insure one-hundred percent of the population against one-hundred percent of the hazards and vicissitudes of life. But we have tried to frame a law which will give some measure of protection to the average citizen and to his family against the loss of job and against poverty-ridden old age ... It is ... a law that will take care of

human needs at the same time provide for the United States an economic structure of vastly greater soundness.

The original act provided only retirement benefits, and only to the worker. The 1939 amendments made a fundamental change in the Social Security program. The amendments added two new categories of benefits: payments to the spouse and minor children of a retired worker (so-called dependents benefits) and survivors' benefits paid to the family in the event of the premature death of the worker.

The most significant change involved the passage of Medicare. Under Medicare, health coverage was extended to Social Security beneficiaries aged sixty-five or older. In a special message to Congress, President Truman proposed a comprehensive, prepaid medical insurance plan for all people through the Social Security system on November 19, 1945. Twenty years later, in July 30, 1965, President Lyndon B. Johnson signed the Medicare Bill in the presence of former President Truman.

Medicare consists of two basic components. Part A is a compulsory hospital insurance (HI) plan that covers a bed patient in a hospital. Part B represents a voluntary program of supplemental medical insurance (SMI) that helps pay doctor bills, outpatient hospital benefits, home health services, and certain other medical services and supplies. It does not cover such things as routine physical examinations, regular eye or hearing examinations, eyeglasses or hearing aids, prescription drugs, false teeth, or full time nursing care.

Social Security is America's family protection plan. Younger workers and their families receive valuable disability and survivors' insurance protection. In fact, about one in three Social Security beneficiaries is not a retiree. A comfortable retirement has always rested on a three-legged financial stool—Social Security, pension, and savings. Today, only a little more than half of all workers have employer-sponsored pensions, and people are not saving as much as they know they should. Most financial advisors say that you'll need 70 percent of preretirement earnings to live comfortably. Even if you can count on a pension, you'll still need to save. If you won't have a private pension, you'll need to save more and start sooner.

Social Security and Medicare are the two great social programs in the United States, but they also bring financial problems to society. The main reason for Social Security's long-range financing problem is demographics. We are living longer lives. When the Social Security program was created in 1935, a sixty-five-year-old had an average life expectancy of 12.5 more years; today, it is 17.5 years and rising. In addition, 77 million baby boomers will begin retiring in about 2010, and in about thirty years, there will be nearly twice as many older Americans as there are today. At the same time, the number of workers paying into Social Security per beneficiary will have dropped. These changes will strain our retirement system.[4]

Neither the founders of Social Security sixty years ago nor the founders of Medicare thirty years ago imagined the demographic shape of America that will unfold over the next several decades. Just pondering the following facts, you will see the seriousness of our entitlement programs[5]:

1. In 1900, only one in twenty-five Americans was over sixty-five. By 2040, one out of every four or five Americans will be over sixty-five. By 2040, the number of "old old" (eighty-five and over) will equal the number of preschool children, according to some forecasts.

2. In 1947, there were no problems because there were slightly more than 22 workers for every recipient. By 1957, the ratio was 5.8 to one, and by 1960 it had fallen to four to one. Today there are 3.3. By 2040, there will be no more than 2.0—and perhaps as few as 1.6. The number of Social Security beneficiaries will at least double by the year 2040.

Table 4.1 Social Security Ratios[5]

Year	Ratio of SS recipient to worker
1947	22 to 1
1957	5.8 to 1
1960	4.0 to 1
2003	3.3 to 1
2040	1.6 to 1

Social Security is taking more in taxes than it is paying out in benefits (in 2000), and the excess funds are credited to Social Security's trust funds. But benefit payment will begin to exceed taxes paid in 2015, and the trust funds will be exhausted in 2037. Comparing Social Security to Medicare, the latter is in worse shape, because Social Security payment to each beneficiary is a fixed amount while the Medicare cost for each patient has no limit. If you can afford Medicare, it is the best health care system in the world, but increasingly, people aren't able to afford it.

Family Caregiving in the United States

Although families play the primary role in maintaining the chronically ill older person at home, these families require outside help in order to sustain such care over time. Studies clearly show that families already provide about 80 percent of all long-term care in the United States. Women represent over 70 percent of all caregivers. In addition, when institutionalization is necessary or unavoidable, families continue to devote considerable time, effort, and emotional energy to their incapacitated kin. Caregiving has become an integral part of the adult life cycle. The "caregiving career" for Alzheimer's disease lasts an average of eight years and may be as long as twenty; because of the extensive burden of care for Alzheimer's disease, the caregiver is commonly described as the disease's "second victim." Moreover, with longer life spans and more sophisticated medical technology, adult children are called upon to provide more intensive care for longer periods than that in the past.

Marital status is an important factor in both the source and the type of informal family support. Males, because they die earlier, generally have a spouse to care for them in the later years. For elderly widows and divorced women, daughters tend to be the primary providers.

Some 1.7 million adult North Carolinians (NCs) are caring for an older person, which is more than 28 percent of NC's adult population. Over 40 percent of NC caregivers care for a person with a memory disorder such as Alzheimer's disease. Family caregivers are the backbone of NC's long-term care system. This is an enormous contribution to the long-term care system. A one-month delay in nursing home placement for persons with Alzheimer's disease is estimated to save Medicare and Medicaid $1 billion. The nationwide economic value of family caregiving in 2000 was estimated to be between $140 and $389 billion.[6] Family caregiving has many rewards, but it can take its toll. It affects the family's routine life and it affects their finances and jobs. All families deserve support for their efforts to provide care. There will be a high price to pay if we do not have family caregiving practice in our health care system.

The formal support system includes a range of health care and social services provided by government agencies, such as a universal health care plan, social welfare, and public transportation. The goals of most government-based support systems are to enable elderly people to remain in their homes as independent citizens and to supplement and complement the informal care provided by families.

The escalating costs associated with caring for an expanding aging population have forced the public and private sectors to shift more of the responsibility for the long-term care of the frail and dependent elderly to individuals and families, or to the private sector. In order that families can assume more of this responsibility, governments and employers have introduced policies to create assistance programs for the caregivers, as well as for the elderly persons.

Most individuals, regardless of age, are never totally isolated from others. The family is the first major source of social support when assistance is needed in the later years. The selection of a preferred caregiver is often made in a hierarchical order, starting with the spouse and followed by an adult child, a sibling, a niece or nephew, and a close friend. The elements of the informal and the formal support systems for older adults should be interlinked to provide a continuum of assistance and care.[7] Family responsibility for caregiving is not a recent issue. The degree of support of an elderly parent or family member is closely related to the sense of obligation and affection built up throughout the family history.

What kind of moral obligation do children have toward the welfare of their elderly parents? Can it be said that the changed health, longevity, and social circumstances of the elderly justify a shift in traditional moral obligations? Even if children do have some significant duties to parents, is it still legitimate to ask the state to take over much of the direct burden of care?

The moral ideal of the parent-child relationship is that of love, nurturing, and mutual concern for the good of the other. Yet the reality of human lives can stand in the way of the realization of moral ideals. Just as not all children are lovable, neither do all parents give the welfare of their children their serious attention and highest priority. Many children do not find their parents lovable and feel no special sense of duty toward them. Many parents are not happy with the way their children have turned out, or with the kind of lives they live, and do not seek to remain intertwined with them.[8]

Older people themselves value personal independence and autonomy. They endeavor not to burden their adult children. The elderly tend to prefer "intimacy at a distance." In fact, affection and closeness actually can dissipate under the real strains of caregiving. Some researchers have found that the stress of excessive caregiver burden can contribute to elder abuse. The use of formal services can actually enhance the relationship between caregivers and care recipients as well as contribute to the latter's dignity. There must be limits to the caregiving burden on adult children and spouses, as well as the option not to provide care.

In promoting individualism and self-reliance, structural management tends to foster dependency. For many older people, the emphasis on individualism and self-reliance also means social isolation. An overemphasis on independence at older ages may be counterproductive. Institutional care is viewed in this country as means of merely maintaining an older person at his or her most basic functioning level.

Families with a senior to take care of should consider all the formal public services available, such as adult day care, in-home aid service, respite care, and so on. North Carolina caregivers with in-home respite or aid services are less likely to place their family members in a long-term care facility than those who receive no aid services. The combination of formal public services and home care is a better approach than doing it alone.

Long-Term Care in the United States

Long-term care can be very costly. The cost of adult care homes (assisted living/rest homes) in Wake County, North Carolina, is $1800 to $4000 per month, depending on the type of facility and level of care required. Nursing facilities may cost $5000 or even more per month. Most people cannot afford the cost of care for an extended period. It has been estimated that long-term care costs will escalate faster than the cost of living, meaning the elderly will be less able to afford home-based services in the future.

On August 27, 2006, The *News & Observer* ran a special report on health care with sensational headline, "Who Can Afford to Be Old and Sick?" According to the report, "there will be a large group of our senior population who will never qualify for public assistance, and yet will never be able to manage the costs they face on a daily basis. Our system fails these people utterly." Mrs. Liz Scott, director of Adult Economic Service in Wake County Human Service, wrote one of the featured articles.

Growing older presents many challenges. Perhaps none is more frightening than the insecurity of how we will pay for what we need. Will we need nursing home care, or will we be able to live independently into our eighties and nineties? Will our Social Security benefits be enough, and will our savings last? Will we have good quality health care that we can afford? The following table breaks down the demographics, by income, of North Carolina households headed by people age sixty-five and older:

Table 4.2 Income of NC Senior Citizens

Amount	Percent
Less than $15,000	29.3 %
$15,000–$29,999	27.9%
$30,000–$44,999	17.3%

Table 4.2 Income of NC Senior Citizens (Continued)

$45,000–$74,999	14.4%
$75,000 and above	11%

For those with higher incomes and significant assets, there are many choices available. For individuals living below the poverty level, there are programs and services available as a safety net. But for those with income above the poverty level and modest savings, there are far fewer choices.

A senior who can no longer live alone must have income below $14,202 per year (this includes Social Security, pensions, etc.) in order to get help paying for the cost of an assisted-living facility. To receive Medicaid for assisted living, an individual can have a monthly income of no more than $1,183.50.

The concept of long-term care has become synonymous with nursing homes. Over 80 percent of all nursing homes are for-profit institutions. As nursing homes have become an increasingly lucrative financial investment, generating high profits, the smaller facilities have gradually disappeared. By 1989, there were more than 16,000 nursing homes, mostly for-profit facilities, providing for 1.5 million elderly.[2]

The hospice program is palliative and not curative in its goals and techniques for helping patients with a life-limiting illness. A hospice is a facility that supports dying persons and their families through a philosophy of "caring" rather than "curing." Hospice entails these key features, which make hospice care different from hospital care:[9]

- The dying person and his or her family—not the experts—decide what support they need and want.

- Attempts to cure the patient or prolong his or her life are de-emphasized. Pain control is emphasized.

- The setting for care is as normal as possible, or at least a home-like facility that does not have the sterile atmosphere of many hospital wards.

- Bereavement counseling is provided to the family before and after the death.

Many patients refuse hospice care until their last days and never take full advantage of the help these programs can provide. Instead, they concentrate on curative medical services and view admission to a hospice program as giving up on living

Asians often ask why American families put their parents into institutions and why a country as rich as the United States does not do more for its elderly people. But in recent years Asia has encountered some of the same problems as western nations in helping a growing population of older citizens. Elderly Chinese people used to take for granted their place in their children's households. But today, although most elderly Asians still live with their children, they are less likely to want to do so than people were in the past, and their children are less prone to urge them to. China is one of several Asian countries that have passed laws obliging people to care for elderly relatives. Institutions are seen as a last resort, to be used only for those elders who are destitute or without families.

A major controversy in Asia, as in the West, is whether housing priority, health care and other social services, and financial aid should be offered to people on the basis of age or of need. What will giving preference mean for the elderly in young families with small children? An aging population could place an unbearable burden on younger generations, with young workers being taxed heavily for pension funds. Or governments may have to cut back services for the young in order to fund services for the old.[10] This is an issue of generational equity.

Directory of Resources

Resources for Seniors, Inc. has made an effort to assist Wake County's elderly population by publishing their annual *Directory of Resources for Old Adults in Wake County*, which includes a comprehensive list of services of particular interest to senior citizens and their families. The mission of Resources for Seniors, Inc. is "to provide home and community based services so that disabled and senior adults can maximize their independence for as long as possible while remaining in their homes." You can get this directory for free at all senior centers and also all North Carolina Department of Health and Human Services offices and their branch offices. I find this directory very helpful. It is the Yellow Pages for senior citizens, and I specially recommend it here in my book.

My Personal Experience and Feelings

Winston Churchill is reported to have said that the quality of any society can be judged in terms of its treatment of and attitudes towards both its elderly and its prison population.[11] In truth, it is easier to manage the problem of death than the problem of living as an old person. In my view, compared with many other nations in the world, our government has done more than its share. The North Carolina Department of Health and Human Services has even established a special organization called the "Division of Aging and Adult Services" to take care of senior citizens. North Carolina has 161 senior centers in 97 of its 100 counties.[12] However, the resources from the tax base should be distributed fairly between the young and the old; I don't think we should ask more than we already have. In my mind, I regard the young as the future of humanity; education for the young should be the primary consideration in any resources distribution at any time.

In order to understand the service available to seniors, I visited quite a few facilities: assisted living, nursing home, and hospice. Perhaps their most striking feature is their drabness. The centers have that "institutional" look shared by police stations, prisons, hospitals, orphanages, and similar public buildings—a nightmarish atmosphere. Even though I have this feeling, I fully understand that the hospice program is very useful to patients with life-limiting illness and their families. The patients may want to be at home, but they may lack the resources they need there. I think that we should take full advantage of the help these programs can provide, including pain and symptom management; home health aid services; and psychological, emotional, and spiritual support.

Before I left the hospice, I asked them, "If I am terminally ill and suffering, should it be my decision or my doctor's when I should die?" They tried to avoid a direct answer but said that they had no choice but to keep the patient alive no matter how the patient is suffering and how much money government has spent without any meaningful result. The patient has no right to make a decision about his or her life. I think this kind of hypocrisy does not benefit the patient or our government. I will talk about this controversial subject in chapter VI.

Notes

1. Laura Katz Olson, *The Graying of the World: Who Will Care for the Frail Elderly?* (New York: The Hawworth Press, 1994), 2–7, 8–15, 22.

2. Ibid., 16–18, 25–31, 42, 51.

3. Social Security Administration, *A Brief History of Social Security,* SSA Publication No. 21-059, August 2000, 3, 7, 10, 15, 19, 20, 21.

4. http://www.ssa.gov/history, May 10, 2006.

5. Social Security Administration. *Social Security: The Future of Social Security.* SSA Publication No. 05-10055, August 2000, 3, 4, 5, 6.

6. http://www.ssa.gov, May 10, 2006.

7. Barry D. McPherson, *Aging as a Social Process* (Toronto, Canada: Harcount Brace & Company, 1998), 331–33.

8. Bowie, Higgins, and Michaels, *Thirteen Questions in Ethics and Social Philosophy,* 2nd ed. (New York: Harcourt Brace College Publishers, 1998), 67–68.

9. Carol K. Sigelman and David R. Shaffer, *Life-span Human Development,* 2nd ed. (Pacific Grove, CA: Brooks/Cole Publishing Company, 1995), 504.

10. D. E. Papalia and S.W. Olds, *Human Development,* 6th ed. (New York: McGraw-Hill, Inc., 1995), 527.

11. Gari Lesnoff-Caravaglia, *Values, Ethics, and Aging* (New York: Human Sciences Press, Inc., 1985), 26.

12. http://www.dhhs.nc.us/aging/scenters/scenters.htm, July 7, 2006.

5

Organization and Function of Senior Centers in North Carolina

Aging North Carolina

North Carolina is in the midst of a significant demographic change as the state's 2.3 million baby boomers enter retirement age in this decade. Today, seniors make up roughly 12 percent of the State's total population; by 2030, the ratio may reach 18 percent, or 2.2 million North Carolinians age sixty-five and over. The following table (based on 2000 U.S Census data) will show the general age characteristics of our State.

Table 5.1 General Characteristics of North Carolina Population[1]

Region	Total population	Population 65 and older	Percentage of population 65 and older (%)
United States	281,421,906	34,991,752	12.4
North Carolina	8,049,313	909,038	12.0
Wake County, NC	627,846	46,372	7.4
Raleigh, NC	276,093	22,995	8.3
Cary, NC	94,536	5,069	5.4
Garner, NC	17,757	1,934	10.9
Wake Forest, NC	12,588	994	7.9

Source: http://www.dhhs.state.nc.us/aging/demo.htm, July 7, 2006.

One of the major factors contributing to the aging of the state is immigration. Migration into North Carolina ranked third nationally, with a net migration of

34,290 among older adults (sixty years and older) between 1995 and 2000. There are other important factors influencing the demographic shifts:

- Rural-to-urban migration of young adults continues to age urban counties.

- Large metropolitan counties attract large numbers of persons from outside the state as well as from rural counties.

- The large metropolitan counties are experiencing greater growth among younger adults than they are among older adults.

- A large number of older adults with higher incomes are retiring in some western and coastal counties.

The aging of the population is a national and international trend, and North Carolina must be prepared to confront the challenge of an older population. Government faces decisions about the allocation of public resources from a tax base that may experience slowed economic growth, especially in many aging counties. People must consider living and caregiving arrangements in light of smaller nuclear and extended families. The business and faith communities must identify and respond to the challenges and opportunities of these demographic shifts.

North Carolina is rich in diversity, but we must face challenges because of the disparity that exists among all populations, including older adults. A survey indicates some important differences among NC's older adults:

- **Gender.** Older women represent 58.8 percent of the sixty-five and older group, and 71.2 percent of the eighty-five-and-older group.

- **Marital status.** At age sixty-five and older, women are more than twice as likely to be unmarried as men in their age group.

- **Ethnicity/race.** Altogether 18.5 percent of persons age sixty-five and older are members of ethnic minority in North Carolina, in which 15.7 percent are African American, 1.0 percent are Latino, and 1.9 percent belong to other ethnic groups.

- **Residence.** In North Carolina, 23.8 percent of all homeowners are age sixty-five and older. Among renters age sixty-five and older, 53 percent spend more than 30 percent of their household income on rent.

- **Disability.** In North Carolina, 44.0 percent of the non-institutionalized civilian population age sixty-five and older reported having one or more disabilities—46.7 percent of women and 40.4 percent of men.

- **Health status.** Heart disease is the leading cause of death among older adults both nationwide and in North Carolina, with cancer and stroke second and third on the list.

To face this challenge of an older population, North Carolina has established the Division of Aging to take care of the aging problem.[2] Senior centers is one of their solutions. The function of a senior center is to serve the recreational, intellectual, and social needs of senior citizens, primarily age fifty-five and over. North Carolina has 161 senior centers in 97 of the counties. They are located in three different areas: 28 percent of centers serve entirely rural areas; 51 percent of all centers are located in towns/cities, but also serve the rural area sounding the town (town and rural); and the remaining 21 percent of centers serve suburban areas. The hierarchy of NC senior centers is quite complicated, but it can be simplified as two parallel systems, shown in Figure 5.1 below.

Figure 5.1 Hierarchy of NC senior centers

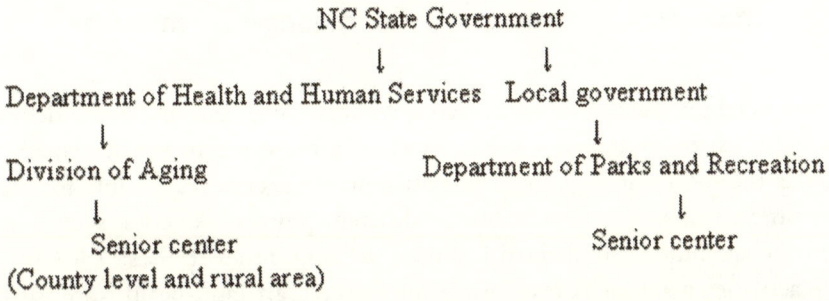

In the 2003–2007 State Aging Plan, the NC Division of Aging and Adults Services introduced a new initiative—Livable and Senior-Friendly Communities—to raise awareness of the aging of our population and to promote North Carolina communities becoming senior-friendly as well as livable for all people. From this plan, we can see that North Carolina has done its best to take care of the welfare of the elderly.

The Organization and Function of Senior Centers

North Carolina has 161 senior centers in 97 of its 100 counties. They are located in three different areas: 28 percent of centers serve entirely rural areas (called rural); 51 percent of all centers are located in towns/cities, but also serve the rural area sounding the town (town and rural); and the remaining 21 percent of centers serve suburban areas, towns, or cities (urban). The structure of a NC senior center is described in the following illustration:[2]

Figure 5.2 Organization of senior center

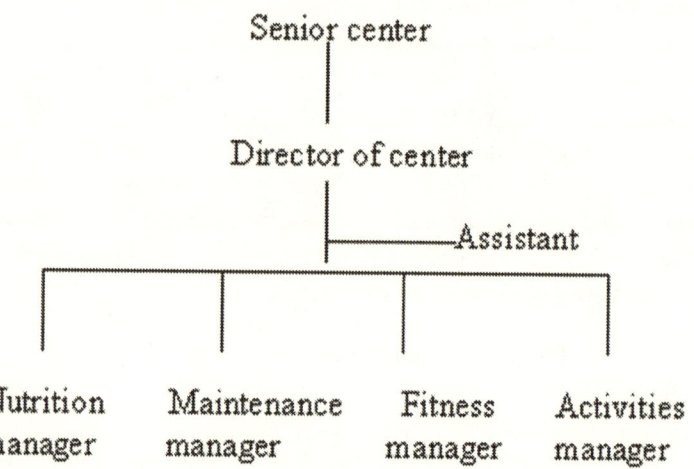

Sixty-eight percent of senior centers offer both congregate and home-delivered meals (lunch only) at a low price, which is a big event in senior centers and attracts the most participants. The nutrition manager is responsible for meals. The fitness manager is responsible for different physical exercises, such as table tennis, chair fitness, shuffleboard, indoor walking, fitness classes, Tai Chi, etc. The activities manager is responsible for cultural, arts and health care, such as book club, card games, bingo, wood carving, rug hooking, movies, trips, and blood pressure check. The factors that affect the processes and activities of NC senior centers are as follows:

1. **Employee and space.** More than a quarter of NC senior centers (26 percent) have only one employee, and the average (mean) number of employees is four. Rural areas are more likely to have centers with only one employee. The average senior center program space (not including offices) is 6,640 square feet.

2. **Attendance.** The average attendance at NC senior centers is 85 people per day. The average attendance is greatest in urban centers and smallest in rural ones.

3. **Budget.** The average senior center budget is $213,305, but the mid-point (median) is only $112,878. Twenty-two percent of the centers have budgets of $50,000 or less. Not surprisingly, centers with more employees have larger budgets. Local government is most likely to fund centers affiliated with public departments of aging and with parks and recreation.

4. **Participants.** "Who comes to the center?" is an interesting question. Thirty-seven percent of senior center participants are in their seventies, and 23 percent are older, including 4 percent who are ninety or older. About 23 percent of senior center participants are men, and the majorities are women. Among the participants at senior centers, about 27 percent are African American. About 8 percent of people who go to senior centers need help to get around (i.e., use a walker, wheelchair, or help from another person).

5. **Activities.** "What do they do there?" is another interesting question. The most popular activities in the senior centers are various kinds of exercises and fitness activities, followed by crafts, trips, cards, and bingo.

6. **Meals-on-wheels.** Sixty-eight percent of centers offer both congregate and home-delivered meals. Only 15 percent have no nutrition programs.

7. **Scheduling.** The average senior center is open nine hours a day. The most common senior center hours are 8:00 a.m. to 5:00 p.m. Monday to Friday. More than half of the centers with evening hours are open three or more times a week. Mornings are the most heavily scheduled times.

8. **Paid personnel.** Staff varies substantially among centers. All centers have a director. The average director is middle aged and has a four-year college degree and many years of experience. The key staff positions are, in order of frequency, support staff, nutrition manager, maintenance personnel, fitness personnel, activities personnel, and assistants.

9. **Strengths and needs.** Centers identify their greatest strengths as their staffs, the variety of activities they offer, and their participants. Space and better transportation are the two most frequently cited needs.

10. **Volunteers.** Most of the 161 centers have volunteers in their centers. The average number of volunteers per center is 109, but 47 percent of

centers have 30 or fewer volunteers. About 82 percent of senior center volunteers are age 60 and older.

The output of senior centers is supposed to serve the recreational, intellectual, and social needs of senior citizens. If they can meet the goal, then we will have healthy senior citizens; in return, the health care cost will be reduced. This is one stone killing two birds—healthy senior citizens and low Medicare cost. Is this output a reality or wishful thinking? Nobody can answer that question with accurate data at this time.

Garner Senior Center

I have been a member of Garner Senior Center since 1996. I have visited quite a few centers, but I think that Garner Senior Center is the largest (in terms of space) and the best (in terms of programs offered and the management).

There was no senior center in Garner before 1990. Mrs. Anna Hudson of Garner has almost single-handedly engineered and executed a major fund-raising drive for the establishment of a senior citizens facility in Garner. Within four years, beginning in 1987, Mrs. Hudson raised $360,000 in cash and $160,000 in services. Due to her dedication and hard work, the knowledge of leaders who could offer assistance, and the enormous amount of time she spent on the project, Garner seniors are seeing their dream come true. The groundbreaking ceremony was held on February 26, 1989, and construction was completed on July 8, 1990. This project has brought the whole community together in an inspiring effort to provide the elderly population of Garner with a building that they can call their own, a place where they can recreate and enjoy fellowship with one another in a comfortable and safe environment. As a member of Garner Center, I am benefited by her effort.

Mrs. Torrey S. Blackmar, director of Garner Senior Center, is busy every day taking care of the senior citizens at the center, but she made time to collect the following statistics for me. From this information, readers can understand the busy schedule of activities in a senior center. These data are daily records in the whole month of August 2006, which cover five categories (represented in the following five tables):

Table 5.3 Residency

Participant	Percentage	Number of people
Resident	51%	787

Table 5.3 Residency (Continued)

Non resident	49%	745

Table 5.4 Race distribution

Race	Number of people	Percentage
Caucasian	1081	71%
African American	292	19%
Unknown	142	9%
Other	21	1%

Table 5.5 Age distribution

Years of birth	Percentage
1900–1905	0%
1906–1910	0%
1911–1915	1%
1916–1920	5%
1921–1925	12%
1926–1930	16%
1931–1935	19%
1936–1940	21%
1941–1945	15%
1946–1950	10%
After 1951	1%

Table 5.6 Age distribution

Age group	Number
55–59	126
60–64	203
65–69	308
70–74	310
75–79	253

Table 5.6 Age distribution (Continued)

80–84	198
85–89	101
90–94	28
95–99	4
100–104	6

Table 5.7 Various programs

Clubs	Times met per month	Number of participants per month
Golden Age Club	1	5
Golden Kiwanis Club	1	8
Joy Club	1	22
Category total	**35**	

Ongoing classes	Meetings	Participants
Bingo	5	185
Board games	6	30
Book club	1	5
Bridge	9	127
Canasta	5	66
Card games	9	91
Chorus	4	65
Movie night	1	15
On the mend	10	123
Pinochle	4	26
Woodcarving	5	17
Piano	3	11
Category total		**761**

Health/fitness		
Badminton	5	43
Basketball	4	6
Beach volleyball	4	6
Beg. table tennis	5	14
Bocce	4	18
Table tennis	9	84
Chair fitness	9	144
Dancercise	4	74
Eve. dancercise	5	54
Fitness classes	14	275
Fitness room use	23	582
Healing touch	2	4
Open gym	4	24
Shuffleboard	5	12
Tops	4	41
Bowling (off site)	2	165
Golf (off site)	5	38
Tennis	8	40
Walking (indoor)	23	233
Women's basketball	5	20
	total	**1877**

Special events and trips	
NC Aquarium at Pine Knoll Shores (Aug 3, 2006)	49
Imax/farmer's market (Aug 25, 2006)	8

Christian Heirs (Aug 17, 2006)		40
Golden Agers shopping trip (Aug 23, 2006)		8
Facials and skin care class (Aug 23, 2006)		20
Category total		**125**
Meals-on-wheels		
Nutrition (congregate) Monday to Friday		1954
Nutrition (home delivery) Monday to Friday		965
Category total		**2919**
Resources for Seniors		
Diabetic support group (Aug 8, 2006)	1	4
ComForCare Sr. Services (Aug 17, 20006)	1	3
Caregiver support group (Aug 17, 2006)	1	1
Blood pressure checks	5	186
Weight checks	5	5
Hearing screenings	1	10
	total	**209**
Monthly Statistics		
Days open		23 days
New registrants		37 people
Rentals		3 times
Town of Garner		5 times

Category	Meetings per month	Participants
Clubs		
Golden Age Club	1	5
Kiwanis Club	1	8
Joy Club	1	22
		Total 35
Ongoing classes		
Bingo etc.	5	185

Grand Total (number of participants)   5994

The grand total, based on three months in the Garner Center, is for reference purposes only. The grand total was 5060 in July, 5994 in August, and 5807 in September. The grand total average of the three months was 5620. This variation is within the statistical margin of error.

Based on 2000 Census data, Raleigh has about 22,995 senior citizens (sixty-five years and over), and Garner has about 1,934 senior citizens, for a total of 24,929. The number 5,994 is about 24 percent of the total 24,929, which means that one of four seniors in Raleigh and Garner areas has visited and used the facilities in the Garner Center. The number of 5,994 is a duplicated number. We can see this statistic from another perspective: 5,994 people divided by thirty days is 199.8 (close to 200). This number means that the average number of participants in the Garner Center is 200 people per day—this is two or three times higher than the average of 85 participants per day in other centers. But this does not mean that 200 different people visit the site each day; the same person may have participated in more than one activity or have gone to the center more than once in a day. Therefore, the unduplicated number of participants may be much less than 200.

My Personal Experience and Feelings

Many older people do not become involved in senior organizations even when such organizations are known and available to them. Those most likely to join are women, those in good health, those with access to transportation, those who have been "joiners" throughout life, those who are members of the lower-middle or middle class, and those with a strong attachment to the neighborhood or community. Those in higher status occupations become more involved in community-centered activities such as service groups and private clubs. The frail elderly, functionally disabled elderly, and ill elderly cannot go; even the well elderly without a car or ride cannot go; only the relatively healthy ones with cars can take full advantage. A lot more needs to be done. I have played table tennis in Garner Center with almost the same players for ten years. I personally feel that the "Senior Center" looks like a semi-private luxury club but built by tax money for healthy elderly.

In a healthy, long-lived culture, many people will question the appropriateness of generous government support based on age when there are so many people of all ages who are desperately needy. Everybody can go to a park or museum, but only people aged fifty-five and over are allowed to go to a senior center, which is built by tax money and is supposed to belong to all the citizens. If a young lawyer brings this case to court, how can the senior center justify its existence legally? It should be renamed "Citizen Center" instead of "Senior Center" to serve all the people. I consider this the greatest problem facing the organization.

Notes

1. http://www.dhhs.state.nc.us/aging/demo.htm, July 7, 2006.

2. Mary Anne P. Salmon, *The Senior Center Capacity Survey*. Report prepared for the Division of Aging and Adult Services, NC, June 2002.

6

Health Care Programs

General Description around the World

The reform of American medical care has been, since at least the fall of 1991, at the very top of the nation's political agenda. But it was the presidential race of 1992—and the presence of a Democratic challenger committed to reforming American medicine—that made the medical care problems of the country front-page news. I think that the comparison of the change in total health care expenditures in several countries will help us understand this problem better:[1]

Table 6.1 Health spending as percentage of GDP, 1970–1990[1]

Country	% of GDP			Percent change 1980–1990
	1970	1980	1990	
United States	7.4	9.3	12.4	33.3
Canada	7.1	7.4	9.0	21.6
Germany	5.9	8.5	8.1	-4.7
France	5.8	7.6	8.9	17.1
Sweden	7.2	9.5	8.7	-8.4
Italy	5.2	6.8	7.6	11.8
Japan	4.4	6.4	6.5	1.5
Britain	4.5	5.8	6.1	4.7

The above chart is comparison of health spending for each nation in the twentieth century; the following one is a comparison of health spending for individuals up to 2002:

Table 6.2 Comparison of health spending for individuals up to 2002[1]

Country	Health expenditure per capita		Total % of GDP
	1991	2002	2002
United States	$2,868	$5,274	14.6
Canada	$1,915	$2,222	9.6
Germany	$1,659	$2,631	10.9
France	$1,650	$2,348	9.7
Sweden	$1,443	$2,489	9.2
Italy	$1,408	$1,737	8.5
Japan	$1,307	$2,476	7.9
Britain	$1,043	$2,031	7.7
Spain	$848	$1,192	7.6
Russia		$150	6.2
China		$63	5.8
India		$30	6.1

Today's Federal Spending

Today, federal spending accounts for more than 20 percent of GDP. About one-third of that spending is devoted to Social Security and Medicare programs aimed at senior citizens, the disabled, and children and spouses of decreased workers. Total education spending, including higher education, consumes less than 3% of the federal budget. The federal government spent a total of $2.2 trillion in 2004, up 5 percent from 2003. Social Security, Medicare, and Medicaid accounted for more than $1 trillion, nearly one-half of total federal spending.[2] The distribution is as follows:

Table 6.3 Health and human services

(including Medicare and Medicaid)	$580.0 billion (26.8%)
Social Security Administration	$531.0 billion (24.6%)
Other agencies	$489.3 billion (22.6%)
National defense	$347.7 billion (16.1%)

Table 6.4 Distribution of federal spending (2006)[3]

Area of spending	Money spent	Percentage of total federal spending (%)
Health and human services (including Medicare and Medicaid)	$580.0 billion	26.8
Social Security administration	$531.0 billion	24.6
Other agencies	$489.3 billion	22.6
National defense	$347.7 billion	16.1

The health care expenditures have almost doubled in ten years, and they will increase even faster as the number of senior citizens increases. No country can afford this trend, no matter how rich they are! This unchecked spending on social programs will trigger recessions and worse.

Table 6.5 Projected distribution of federal spending

Year	Social Security	Medicare	Deficit
2005	$514 billion	$336 billion	$319 billion
2050	$1.99 trillion	$2.67 trillion	$4.62 trillion

This hidden debt equals $473,456 per household, which the government isn't asking you to pay yet. According to a Web site sponsored by the US government, "Without major spending cuts, tax increases, or both, the national debt will grow more than $3 trillion through 2010 to $11.2 trillion—nearly $38,000 for every man, woman, and child. The interest alone would cost $561 billion in 2010, the same as the Pentagon."[3] Someday and somehow, the future generations will have to pay. There is no free lunch.

Medical Care Reform Proposals

Sensible health care reform should build on three fundamental principles: cost, access, and quality. These principles are interconnected, and we cannot solve one problem without attending to the other two. More than 70 percent of Americans in a public opinion poll agreed that American medicine needed either fundamental change or complete rebuilding. Commentators generally divide major medical care reform proposals into three groups:[4]

1. **Pay-or-play proposals** would compel employers to provide health insurance for employees and their dependents, or pay a tax into a publicly-funded plan to cover them.

2. **Single-payer proposals** aim to provide universal coverage through a single government insurance plan, which is the key feature of the Canadian system of insurance.

3. **Pro-competitive proposals** explicitly reject the Canadian approach of controlling costs through negotiated budgets for hospitals and fee schedules for doctors. Instead, these reform proposals hope to restrain medical inflation by fostering increased competition between doctors, hospitals, and insurance plans.

The central questions of these proposals are whether and how medical care should be rationed, what the potential is for eliminating waste and inefficiency in the provision of care, how to use competition versus regulation in controlling costs, and whether there is a right to medical care.

Is Medicare a right? The answer is not at all clear; capitalists and socialists each have their own arguments. In the capitalist view, medical care is not like food and shelter, which are basic prerequisites for life; medical care is a luxury, and Medicare is an egalitarian (socialist) program. But almost all Americans agree that medical care should not be allocated primarily on the basis of ability to pay, and that everyone should receive a decent minimum standard of care. Of course, some people can afford better health insurance than others.

No one seriously doubts that American medical care needs reform. The most obvious problems are skyrocketing costs. What most citizens and many experts want from a modern system of medical care seems desirable, but they may be impossible in a market economy:

- Universal coverage for all Americans with no deductibles or co-payment obligations

- Universal insurance for all medically necessary care

- Freedom to choose one's doctors, hospitals, and individual treatment without bureaucratic hassles

- Portable insurance that follows the citizen and is not tied to a specific job or locale

Dialectically speaking, the Medicare program and its reforms cannot please either side. On the one hand, the health care system wants to make money, and on the other, the patients complain about the high price but want to live long at any cost.

Medicare insurance is a national system of financing individual health services on a social insurance basis. Because Medicare and Medicaid result from legal entitlements to services, there has been some concern that expenditures from these programs are uncontrollable. The costs of providing medical care under these programs have increased at a rate exceeding the growth of the federal economy and the consumer price index. Health care costs have exceeded national defense costs since 1994.

Senior citizens as a block have voting power, and no politicians dare to touch the entitlement programs. As time goes on, the situation will get worse, and on our present course we won't be able to afford it. As a senior citizen myself, I have the advantage to speak out without being called biased and unfair. Before too late, we had better face the Medicare problem honestly, and the time to act is now.

Just what is it that we want medicine to do for us as we age? In my opinion, the goal of medicine in the care of the aged should be improving the quality of their life, not seeking ways to extend that life. To do otherwise would harm the needs of other age groups and the old themselves. A plan to limit health care for the aged under public entitlement programs that is fair, humane, and sensitive to their special requirements and dignity has to follow three principles:[5]

1. Government has a duty to help people live out a natural life span, but not actively to help medically extend life beyond that point.

2. Government is obliged to develop under its research subsidies and pay for, under its entitlement programs, only that kind and degree of life-extending technology necessary for medicine to achieve and serve the end of a natural life span.

3. Beyond the point of natural life span, government should provide only the means necessary for the relief of suffering, not life-extending technology. The future of our society will not be served by allowing expenditures on health care for the elderly endlessly and uncontrollably to escalate.

In the name of medical progress we have waged a relentless war against death and decline, failing to ask in any probing way if that will give us a better society for all age groups. The proper question is not whether we are succeeding in giving a longer life to the aged. It is whether we are ensuring old age is a decent and honorable time of life. Neither a longer lifetime nor more life-extending technology is the way to that goal.

Comparative Study of Health Care Cost

Many American senior citizens go to Canada or Mexico to buy drugs or order them by mail, resulting in a type of border war. The border war is being driven by a rapid rise in the cost of medications and the frustration of one in four seniors who have no drug coverage. According to the front-page report in *USA Today*, October 7, 2003, people in the United States pay higher prices for the same prescription drugs than do residents of other industrialized countries. The following diagrams and numbers show how much more Americans have paid than people in those countries:

Table 6.6 Health costs in Europe (Americans pay more than ...)

Switzerland	by	58%
Great Britain	by	60%
Canada	by	67%
Germany	by	74%
Sweden	by	78%
France	by	102%
Italy	by	112%

Table 6.7 Comparing U.S. and Canada prescription drug prices (same dosage and quantity)

Drug	Treatment	U.S.	Canada	Savings	%
Casodex	Prostate cancer	$403.99	$237.78	$166.21	59%
Coumadin	Prevents blood clots	$99.99	$56.42	$43.58	56%
Dilantin	Seizures	$27.99	$23.50	$4.49	84%
Glucophage	Diabetes	$135.99	$112.01	$23.98	82%
Permax	Parkinson's	$211.99	$133.63	$78.36	63%

Table 6.7 Comparing U.S. and Canada prescription drug prices (same dosage and quantity) (Continued)

Prednisone	Allergies	$42.29	$33.36	$8.93	79%
Tamoxifen	Breast cancer	$61.99	$52.95	$9.04	85%
Vioxx	Arthritis and pain	$91.99	$56.36	$35.62	61%
Wellbutrin	Depression	$109.99	$27.53	$82.46	75%
Zocor	High cholesterol	$51.99	$28.76	$23.23	55%

This price structure difference between neighbor countries is unsustainable, unforgivable, and intolerable. This is a good example of how private business in the capitalist world acts in its own interest, and not for its citizen's welfare. Besides the drug price differences, the United States also utilizes more expensive technology in health care, which may be not necessary. The following chart is an example.

Table 6.8 Costs of medical technology

Medical technology	U.S.	Canada	Ratio
Open-heart surgery	3.26	1.23	2.7:1
Cardiac catheterization	1.50	5.06	3.4:1
Organ transplantation	1.31	1.08	1.2:1
Radiation therapy	3.97	0.54	7.4:1
Magnetic resonance imaging	3.69	0.64	8.0:1

Seniors are not happy with the high drug costs in the United States. During the 2002 election campaign, the powerful pharmaceutical industry gave $22 million to political candidates. George Bush was its top recipient, collecting nearly $500,000. The drug industry is one of the most powerful lobbies in Washington. It employs hundreds of lobbyists, more than one for every member of Congress. One of these lobbyists is Tony Feather, who was political director of the Bush-Cheney campaign in 2000.[6]

Americans pay the highest prices for drugs in the world. The same drug sold at a high price in the United States, but is sold at an average 65 percent lower price in countries with price-control laws in place. There is no evidence of a single case of anybody getting ill from legitimate Canadian drugs. In fact, many drugs are manufactured in the United States, exported to Canada, and mail ordered back by patients because the drug prices are lower in Canada. At present, Congress is considering legalizing "re-importation," since drugs sold abroad are made by American companies.[7]

The issue of buying lower cost medicines from abroad is rapidly escalating into a major revolt against high U.S. prescription drug prices, as local and state governments defiantly challenge the pharmaceutical industry and the Bush administration. The city of Springfield, Massachusetts, is already buying from Canada for the city's active and retired workers. The city's annual prescription drug costs have more than doubled, to $18 million, over the past eight years. Buying at Canada prices could save up to $9 million a year. Illinois spent $340 million last year on prescription drugs for its 230,000 state employees and retirees. They estimate that if they go to Canada, they can get the same drug made by the same company for half the price.[7]

All industrialized countries have their own version of the Food and Drug Administration (FDA) to monitor and control the quality of food and drug products and to protect their citizens. The lives of the citizens in other countries are just as valuable as American lives. If each country has no confidence in the others' regulation, safety, and ability to do a good job, they should stop all exports and imports. To use an analogy, many foreign tourists drive cars on our crowded highways with foreign driver's licenses. This situation is more dangerous than importing drugs, because a single automobile can cause a chain accident and kill many people.

To solve the dilemma of drug importation, the government has to negotiate with foreign governments to reach a reciprocal agreement, mutually respect each other's ability and sincerity, check the products, and supervise the practice. Doing so will open many doors for international competition, such as foreign hospital operation and pharmaceutical manufacturing in U.S. and vice versa, which will eventually keep down the cost of Medicare.

My Personal Experience, Feelings, and Suggestions

Is American medical care reform doomed to fail? It is very hard to see a clear answer, which depends on the mentality and attitude of the people. The Medicare program is a typical example of interest conflict and ideological war. The business of the health care system, including pharmaceutical industry and hospitals, is to make money. International competition can be bad for corporate business; therefore, corporations have used "safety" as a justification to block foreign companies from entering into the domestic market. Furthermore, the expansion of the health system's bureaucracy, the growth of the population, and patients' unrealistic demand for a long life, combined, have pushed health care costs beyond control.

Most reform proposals about Social Security and Medicare are in the area of Social Security tax and Social Security Trust Fund management. These proposals are useful in keeping the Medicare program in operation for the time being, but they are not the permanent solution.

The aim of medicine is to preserve human health and to cure illness in human beings, not to prolong patients' lives forever at any cost. Medicare is health care insurance, not life insurance. In medical practice, I would like to suggest five proposals for consideration:

1. If a patient is suffering with terminal illness, especially a senior citizen, the patient should have the basic human right to choose his or her own destination: euthanasia or continuing suffering. This must occur on a strict voluntary basis, without any coercion or legal restriction. Medicare spends lots of its budget on patients often when the attempt to prolong life merely prolongs a hospitalized death.

2. A living will should be required by law and verified at driver license application; it should also be encouraged by monetary incentive. Eliminating unnecessary and unwanted life-support practice alone can save lots of money in Medicare costs.

3. There should be a rational limitation on what medical treatment is allowed for what age. For example:

   a. Organ transplant may be limited to individuals under sixty-five years of age. This rule will give young people a chance to finish business in their remaining time; besides, there are not enough organs available to meet all needs.

   b. Open-heart surgery or cancer treatment may be limited to individuals below 90 or 95 years of age or at any age limit. Few senior citizens get cancer at very old age, if they do, it is too late to cure. Medicare cannot work miracles.

   c. Patients should be allowed to buy drugs across borders if the drug price in another country is cheaper. We have to remember that each country has its own version of the FDA to control quality and safety. We should treat others as equal partners, with respect.

4. In a free-market economy, the market should open to international competition to benefit the consumers. The powerful pharmaceutical industry should not be allowed to control the market and to make excessive profit at the expense of ill patients.

5. The hospital system should also open to international competition under strict legal supervision. Allowing foreign hospitals to operate under the same quality standard as the United States will save money in Medicare insurance. I will emphasize that nothing can help Medicare reduce its costs more than international competition.

We need bold actions to remove the obstacles to meeting the health care needs of the elderly. Will people accept that death always occurs after birth takes place? Will medical practice be for the benefit of patients, not for capitalist profit? Will people accept that Medicare is health care insurance, not life insurance? Do we have the courage to ask for the right to die? Do we have our natural right to be free? Without honest answers to these questions, we cannot solve the Medicare dilemma.

USA Today, ABC News, and the Kaiser Family Foundation conducted a wide-ranging national telephone survey in early September 2006. The poll found a growing unease in America about the rising cost of health care, confusion about the causes of this trend, and a desire for major reform. But it also found distaste for giving anything up to achieve sweeping changes. An overwhelming 80 percent of respondents said they were dissatisfied with the total tab the nation spends on health care, estimated to hit $2.2 trillion, or $7,129 a person, a year.[8]

American voters repeatedly elect leaders who promise lower taxes, higher benefits, rejuvenated economic growth, and a magic bullet for every social problem—without caring how to implement their promises. Empty promises cannot solve the Medicare dilemma; Medicare needs money. Without resources, the insurance companies and the health care system will gradually cut corners to protect its own interest, whether patients like it or not.

With limited tax dollars, vast senior population growth, and skyrocketing medical costs, the Medicare program and the health care insurance companies will eventually have to take bold actions as proposed above, implicitly or explicitly, to avoid bankruptcy. The easiest and the most efficient Medicare reform to implement is to open the market and adopt free international competitions in all fields, which will bring the greatest good for the greatest number and do the least harm. Changing the Medicare program is a not a possibility but a necessity; it is just a matter of time. But I doubt my above three suggestions will be considered soon, for the following reasons:

1. Letting foreign investors invest in the pharmaceutical industry and hospital operation will affect American profits.

2. Letting terminally ill patients have the right to die will affect hospitals' profit.

3. Establishing rational limitations on what medical treatments are available at what age will affect hospitals' and the pharmaceutical industry's profit, and a human rights violation.

We cannot understand the health system without understanding the entire economy, of which it is but one sector. No analysis of the health sector in isolation is of any value, because it does not reflect reality. Similarly, we cannot presume to change the health system to the benefit of the masses without engaging in the overall social class struggle. Discussions of reform confined to the health system alone are pure fantasy.[9] Dialectically speaking, Medicare program and its reform cannot please either side. On the one hand, the health care system wants to make money, and on the other, the patient complains about the high price but wants to live long at any cost.

Furthermore, Medicare is health care insurance for aged people only; what we need the most is national health care insurance for all ages—especially for the young, the future of our society. We know very well that a car without regular preventive maintenance cannot last long; the same is true for human beings. Without good health care in youth, one cannot have a healthy body at old age. National health care insurance is really the preventive maintenance of all citizens' health, and it will reduce the cost of health care (including Medicare) in the long run.

Notes

1. Theodore R. Marmor, *Understanding Health Care Reform,* (New Haven: Yale University Press, 1994), 2, 3, 14.

2. http://www.seniorjournal.com, May 20, 2006.

3. http://www.nationalprioities.org, May 20, 2006.

4. Theodore R. Marmor, *Understanding Health Care Reform,* (New Haven: Yale University Press, 1994), 123–33, 147, 188.

5. Bowie, Higgins, and Michaels. *Thirteen Questions in Ethics and Social Philosophy,* 2nd ed. (New York: Harcourt Brace College Publishers, 1998), 666–70.

6. *USA Today,* October 7, 2003.

7. AARP, *AARP Bulletin* 44:10 (November 2003), 3–4.

8. *USA Today,* October, 16, 2006.

9. Marlene Dixon and Thomas Bodenheimer, ed., *Health Care in Crisis.* (New York: Synthesis Publication, 1980), 1–6.

7

Dying, Death, and Euthanasia

This chapter will focus on some ethical issues closely related to senior citizens. I consider this the most important chapter in this book, and I will present these issues in detail from a philosophical perspective. First I will discuss the meaning of the three terms, and then I will argue for the right to die.

What Is Death?

Death, the date and circumstances of which are set by God alone, is the limit to man. We, with the limited power of science and technology, should never abuse God's power. Death always has been and always will be with us. It is an integral part of human existence. Man's existence is characterized by temporality. Death can only occur after birth takes place. Death comes to all men and women, and death spares no one. It makes all men equal. We cannot apprehend death in its own terms. Death is mute, and it renders us speechless. As long as we are alive, we cannot expect death itself to provide the answer on the question of death. None of us knows what awaits us after this life. Dr. Ludwig Wittgenstein, a German thinker, said, "Death is not an event in life; we do not live to experience death." Death is part of the form and structure in which life is given.[1]

Human development is growth in early life and aging in later life, which is the deterioration of organisms that leads inevitably to their death. It used to be easy enough to tell that someone was dead: there was no breathing, no heartbeat (no blood pressure), rigidity of the body, and no sign of responsiveness. These criteria of biological death are still useful today. However, technological breakthroughs have forced the medical community to rethink what it means to say that someone is dead. In 1968, an ad hoc committee of Harvard Medical School offered a definition of death that it hoped would resolve controversies about when a person is dead. The Harvard group defined biological death as total brain death, which must meet the following criteria:[2]

- Be totally unresponsive to stimuli, including painful ones.

- Fail to move for one hour and fail to breathe for three minutes after being removed from a ventilator.

- Have no reflexes. The pupil will be fixed and dilated and will not respond to a direct source of bright light.

- Register a flat electroencephalogram (EEG), indicating an absence of electrical activity in the cortex of the brain.

- As an additional precaution, the testing procedure is repeated twenty four hours later.

In 1981, a presidential commission voted that a Uniform Determination of Death Act be adopted by all states, an action endorsed by the American Medical Association and the American Bar Association. The act reads, "An individual who has sustained either (1) irreversible cessation of circulatory or respiratory function, or (2) irreversible cessation of all function of the entire brain, including the brain stem, is dead. A determination of death must be made in accordance with accepted medical standards."[3]

Our image of death has been transformed from death as a natural event (not to be fought), to death as a force of nature (to be avoided), to death as something caused by specific disease, to society's obligation to fight the unnatural death of all of its members, and to an all-out war against death. Thus, although death was once recognized as a natural part of the living process, it has come to be viewed as an evil to be avoided and fought at every step and at any cost. This includes the use of highly sophisticated life-support systems capable of keeping people "alive" in intensive care units, patients who would surely die without such devices. A person should not be treated merely as a means to an end even when that end is one that the person accepts.

We all wish to have an appropriate death, which means dying as we wish to die. Permitting individuals an appropriate death allows them to maintain a sense of hopefulness—the positive anticipation of the future—which provides a sense of control of mastery. In a good or appropriate death, the dying person is able to bring life to an orderly close, and the final stage of life contributes to personal growth. Most people try to maintain as much control over their dying as possible to render it meaningful. This involves completing unfinished business, such as saying farewell as well as making a will, funeral plans, and other arrangements for survivors after death.[4]

Maria Reynolds said, "There is some fear—not of death, but of what one must become before death. Death in itself is nothing; but we fear to be we know not what, we know not where." The stark truth is that all patients dying of old age must expect, as a matter of routine, to be forced through an additional period, sometimes a long period, of pain and/or acute discomfort before death finally comes.[5]

If death is the unequivocal and permanent end of our existence, the question arises whether it is a bad thing to die. Some people think death is dreadful because it brings to an end all the good that life contains; others have no objection to death per se, although they hope their own will be neither premature nor painful. It is the quality of life that counts and not the number of years we live. Quality of life and death with dignity are the concerns of patients. Quality of life is the end, but a mere low-level existence is definitely not. It is sometimes suggested that what we really mind is the process of dying, not death.[6]

The Dying Process

The process of dying is a process of recommitment to life, coming out of a new situation. There are patterns of how people undergoing the most important transcendent experience of their lives—living with the imminent reality of death—respond to themselves, to their situations, and to others in those situations. According to Kubler-Ross, dying persons experience five stages in reaction to their death:[7]

1. **Denial and isolation.** The dying person may deny what he or she really feels to avoid punishment.

2. **Anger and resentment.** Anger (why me?) may be displaced on family or medical staff and can lead to withdrawal and avoidance. This stage may be the most difficult for caregivers to tolerate.

3. **Bargaining and an attempt to postpone.** The dying person may try to make a deal with God to live long enough to attain some goal or to postpone death as a reward for good behavior.

4. **Depression and sense of loss.** The dying person may withdraw from loved ones as a way to prepare for this separation.

5. **Acceptance.** The dying person thereby achieves a sense that personal tasks have been accomplished and the struggle is over. Rather than a happy stage, the acceptance stage is almost devoid of feelings and should not be confused with wishing to die.

Kubler-Ross emphasizes that dying can be a time of growth. By accepting death's inevitability, dying persons can use life meaningfully and productively and come to terms with who they really are. Since the dying are "our best teachers," those who work with them can learn from them and emerge from such experiences with fewer anxieties about their own dying. Death is the key to the door of life—as a caterpillar becomes a butterfly.[7]

Euthanasia—The Right to Die

Choosing a "good death," which is a literal translation of euthanasia, is usually thought to be justifiable when death is at hand, as in terminal illness. We are not morally obliged to preserve life in all terminal cases. Given modern medicine's capabilities, to do what is technically possible to prolong life in every case would be morally indefensible on any ground other than a vitalistic outlook. The traditional ethics based on the sanctity of life, which was the classical doctrine of medical idealism in its pre-scientific phases, must give way to an ethics of the quality of life.

A careful typology of elective death will distinguish at least five forms—five ways of dying that are not blind chance but matters of choice, purpose, and responsible freedom:[8]

1. **Active, voluntary, direct.** This is death chosen and carried out by the patient. It is a simple request for personal liberty. In a word, it is suicide.

2. **Passive, voluntary, direct.** The choice might be made in situation or long in advance of a terminal illness, e.g., by exacting a promise that if and when the patient cannot be self-administered, somebody will do it for the patient.

3. **Passive, voluntary, indirect.** This is done for rather than by the patient, but with his consent and by indirect means only. A directive or form called the living will is in wide use, with legal enforcement in some states.

4. **Passive, involuntary, direct.** This is the form or procedure in which a simple "mercy killing" is done on a patient's behalf without his present or prior consent.

5. **Passive, involuntary, indirect.** This is the act of "letting the patient go," which often happens in our health care system.

Dr. Leslie Weatherhead, the revered former minister of the City Temple in London, wrote, "I sincerely believe that those who come after us will wonder why on earth we kept a human being alive against his own will, when all the dignity, beauty and meaning of life had vanished; when any gain to anyone was clearly impossible, and when we should have been punished by the State if we kept an animal alive in similar physical conditions."[9] People, like animals, have a legal and moral right to a merciful death, or euthanasia. Such a basic right seems especially relevant now, when our doctors are able to exercise an ever-increasing range of professional choices to elongate life. Dr. G. B. Giertz, the president of the Swedish Society of Surgery, said,

> The thought that we physicians should be obliged to keep a patient alive with a respirator when there is no possibility of recovery, solely to try to prolong his life by perhaps twenty-four hours, is a terrifying one. It must be regarded as a medical axiom that one should not be obliged in every situation to use all means to prolong life. We restrain from treatment because it does not serve any purpose, because it is not in the patient's interest. I cannot regard this as killing by medical means; death has already won, despise the fight we have put up, and we must accept the fact.[9]

Presumably no society can survive if it allows its members to kill one another without restriction. Just who is protected, however, is a matter on which societies have differed. Nowadays most agree that it is wrong to kill human beings irrespective of their race, religion, class, or nationality. But the question of whether voluntary euthanasia should be legal has not been answered. Before looking at the ethical issue of euthanasia, we must first know where moral standards come from. Only then can we argue what is right and wrong.

Morality and Ethics

Ethics deals with individual behavior; politics deals with community. Ethics is not law. The legality of an action does not guarantee that the action is morally right. In theory and practice, law codifies a society's customs, ideas, norms, and moral values. From the sociological perspective, ethical codes we employ were selected because they enhanced long-term group survival and harmony. Ethical theory is just an intellectual opinion; the truth of an opinion is part of its utility. If we are to act morally, we must follow the same moral rules in dealings with others that we expect them to follow in their dealings with us. Morality is a two-way street.

Ethical theory covers a very wide field in philosophy. For philosophers, the important question is not how we came to have the particular principles we have. The philosophical issue is whether the principles we have can be justified. In order to illustrate the key point of ethics, I would like to simplify it into three groups:

1. **Divine command theory.** If something is wrong, then the only reason it is wrong is that God commands us not to do it. According to the divine command theory, there is no reason that something is right or wrong other than it being God's will. Morality is based on the commands of God, although a desire to avoid hell and to go to heaven may prompt some of us to act morally. An act is right if and only if God commands it.[10] As far as Christians are concerned, their guide is the Bible, whereas Muslims follow the Koran and Buddhists have their sutras. So you see, even divine command is not absolute.

2. **Teleological ethical theory.** This ethical doctrine holds that the consequences of a moral act determine the act's worth and correctness. One may have the best intentions or follow the highest moral principles, but if the result of a moral act is harmful or bad it must be judged as a morally or ethically wrong act. This theory instructs us to produce the best consequences.

   John Stuart Mill (1806–1873) was a leading exponent of *utilitarian moral philosophy*. Its main tenet is the "greatest happiness" principle: one should act as to promote the greatest happiness (pleasure) for the greatest number of people. The moral worth of an act is judged according to the balance of good over evil of its consequences. The greatest happiness principle holds that actions are right in proportion as they tend to promote happiness and wrong as they tend to produce the opposite of happiness.[11] The utilitarian doctrine advocates that happiness is desirable, and the only thing desirable as an end; all other things are desirable only as means to that end. Furthermore, utilitarianism concerns itself with the sum total of happiness produced, not with how that happiness is distributed.

   Sometimes Jesus himself is interpreted as adhering to utilitarianism, such as when he breaks the Sabbath laws in order to do good, saying that "the Sabbath was made for man, not man for the Sabbath" (Mark 2:27). We might well paraphrase Jesus, saying, "Morality and law were made for man, not man for morality and law."[12] What good was adherence to outworn moral rules that served no useful purpose and kept the poor from enjoying a better life?

Utilitarianism has two main features: the consequentialist principle (or its teleological aspect) and the utility principle (or its hedonic aspect).[12] The consequentialist principle states that the rightness or wrongness of an act is determined by the goodness or badness of the results that flow from it. It is the end, not the means, that counts. The end justifies the means. The utility principle states that the only thing that is good in itself is some specific type of state (e.g., pleasure, happiness, or welfare).

Utilitarianism does have two positive characteristics. The first attraction or strength is that it is a system with a single absolute principle, with a potential answer for every situation. ("Do what will promote the most utility!") The second strength is that utilitarianism seems to get at the substance of morality. It is not merely a formal system, offering only formal principles, but has a material core—promoting human and animal happiness and ameliorating suffering. The first virtue gives one a clear decision procedure for arriving at our answer about what to do. The second virtue appeals to our sense that morality is made for human (and other animals) and that it is not so much about rules as about helping people and alleviating the suffering in the world.[12]

However, utilitarianism has problems that must be addressed before one can give it a clean bill of health. How can we know the consequences of actions? Sometimes utilitarians are accused of playing God. They seem to hold to an ethical theory that demands godlike powers, that is, knowledge of the future.[12]

3.   **Deontological ethical theory.** This ethical doctrine holds that the worth of an action is determined as by its conformity to some binding rules rather than by its consequences. Teleological ethics instructs us to produce the best consequences; deontological ethics instructs us to follow the correct rules regardless of the consequences. Their difference is like day and night.

Immanuel Kant (1724–1804) incorporated the basic idea of the Golden Rule into his system of ethics. Kant argued that we should act only on rules that we are willing to have everyone follow. He held that there is one supreme principle of morality, which he called the *categorical imperative*.[13] Kant maintained that what makes an action morally right is that we can will it to be a universal law. We now have two ways of reformulating his categorical imperative that may be easier to grasp and apply:[14]

a.   **The Formula of the Law of Nature.** Act as if the maxim of your action will become through your will a universal law of nature.

b.   **The Formula of the End in Itself.** Act in such way that you always treat humanity, whether in your own person or in the person of any other, never simply as a means but always at the same time as an end.

Let us discuss what these two formulas mean. First, when we are trying to decide whether we ought to do a certain action, we must first ask what general rule or principle we would be following if we did it. Then we ask whether we would be willing for everyone to follow that rule in similar circumstances. (This determines whether "the maxim of the act"—the rule we would be following—can be willed to be "a universal law.") If we would not be willing for the rule to be followed universally, then we should not follow it ourselves. Thus, if we are not willing for others to apply the rule to us, we ought not to apply it to them.

Second, what makes an action right is that the agent treats human beings as ends in themselves. For example, Kant believed that prostitution is immoral because, by selling their sexual services, prostitutes allow themselves to be treated as means. The foundation of this principle is that rational nature exists as an end in itself—it is an objective end. If, now, the action is good only as a means to something else, then the imperative is hypothetical.

Nothing, Kant said, is good in itself except a good will. Kant believed that anything's goodness depends on the will that makes use of it. By "will," Kant meant the uniquely human capacity to act from principle. Contained in the notion of good will is the concept of duty: only when we act from duty does our action have moral worth. When we act only out of feeling, inclination, or self-interest, our actions—although they may be otherwise identified with ones that spring from the sense of duty—have no true moral worth. According to Kant, if you do not will the action from a sense of your duty to be fair and honest, your action does not have true moral worth. But then what determines our duty? How do we know what morality requires of us? What makes a moral act right? Kant answered these questions by formulating the categorical imperative.[15] (Act as if the maxim of your action were to become, by the will, a universal law of nature.)

A good will is good not because of what it performs or effects but simply by virtue of the volition; that is, it is good in itself. Like a jewel, it would still shine by its own light, as a thing which has its own value. Its usefulness or fruitlessness can neither add to nor take away anything from this value. I am never to act otherwise except that I could also will that my maxim should become a universal law.

The principle of beneficence is both teleological and consequential. It is teleological because it involves pursuing good for others. It is consequential because it considers the effects of actions on the welfare of others. A major difficulty in its application is the necessity for prediction and assessment of outcomes. Some philosophers—you might call them mixed-deontologists—would combine deontological ethics with consequentialism, holding that we ought to follow the rules in general, since they have strong presumptive force, but override them with the principle of beneficence where great good can be accomplished. Both deontological and consequentialist ethics have important insights. The question is, "How do we best incorporate these insights into a unified ethical theory?"[16]

Summary of Morality and Ethics

As moral decision makers, we are seeking not just an answer to a moral issue but an answer that can be publicly defended. And the public defense of a moral judgment usually requires an appeal to general principle. We cannot sincerely endorse a principle if we are not willing to see it applied generally. Most versions of utilitarianism and Kantian ethics are rule oriented and embrace either some version of the maximization principle or the principle of universalizability.

At the base of these theories concerning what we ought to do lies the distinction between morality and prudence. Morality tells us what our duties and obligations are, regardless of our individual interests, while prudence tells us what we should do if we are to serve our interests. Theories of duty and obligation are either teleological theories, specifying duty in terms of the maximization of pleasure, utility, happiness, etc., for the greatest number; or they are deontological theories specifying duty in terms of the universalizability of one's maxims.

Morality's value is not based on the fact that it has instrumental value, that it often secures non-moral goods such as happiness, but that it is valuable in its own right. Moral duty must be done solely for its own sake (duty for duty's sake).

John Stuart Mill said in his famous book *On Liberty*, "Unless the reasons of the theory are good for an extreme case, they are not good for any case." Kant said that a moral rule must function without exception. Of course this is right in theory; in reality, no ethical rule is free of exception. For example, lying is wrong because it treats others as merely means to your own ends; however, in our life we find sometimes that lying is not only necessary but also beneficial to all concerned.

Do we take into equal account everybody's happiness before we act? Splurging on presents for our families may be wrong because we might create greater happiness by spending our money on the poor instead. These examples indicate that no ethical theory is perfect; no one fundamental moral principle can underlies all of morality. This is a dilemma in the application of ethical rules.

Argument on Euthanasia from an Ethical Perspective

Morality is more than a matter of rules in that it inescapably involves questions of meaning in human life, of human nature, and of our overall aims and ideals. If one has overall aims in life and thinks that one's life leads up to something, then one can entertain hope even under adverse circumstances; these aims enable us to find acceptance of conditions beyond our control (e.g., aging, death).[17]

By the categorical imperative, euthanasia is justified because the patients do not want the doctors use them as means. The patient is a rational being; a rational being exists as an end in itself. The patient's end is quality of life, not low-level of existence by life-sustaining treatment. An objective end is the right to choose even to die. From the standpoint of reducing suffering, I adopt it as a principle to shorten my life when its longer duration is likely to bring more evil than satisfaction. It is asked then simply whether this principle founded on reducing suffering can become a universal law of nature. If it can, then euthanasia is justified. We should act in such a way that we can will the maxim of our action to become a universal law.

If the maxim is to prolong the process of dying without any hope of cure, if the doctor's maxim is to keep a patient alive even if only in a vegetable existence, can the maxim really become a universal law of nature? Can the doctor's action of keeping a human being in vegetable existence be compatible with the idea of humanity as an end in itself? Is the vegetable existence the end of humanity? Is prolonging the process of dying the end itself? At any given moment, will an act in such a way promote the greatest good for the greatest number? By this rule, euthanasia may be justified because it will reduce the burden to family and society and promote the greatest good for the greatest number. As a rational being, the patient must choose the course of action that has the best consequences, or balance, for all affected.

If there are any moral rights at all, there is at least one prior right founded on justice—the equal right of all persons to be free to decide for themselves. A just society is here distinguishable from one that is unjust. An unjust society makes no provision for the physically weak and infirm to have their moral rights respected and recognized and put into effect. A just society is one that respects a person's inviolable right to be free even if he is in no position to make the needed physical movements to assume and safeguard his rights. Only the patient has the moral right to decide the question of his death and to ensure that his right to live or die shall be respected. Every person has the equal right to be free to decide to live or die, just as he or she has the equal right to be free and to be treated fairly and impartially.[18]

Argument on Euthanasia from the Medical Perspective

When a patient is severely ill, he is often treated like a person with no right to an opinion. What man needs most is to feel secure in his self-esteem, the right to be heard. This security is not afforded to a seriously ill patient. It is often someone else who makes decisions for the patient. Decisions are often made without his opinion. He is no longer a person. He will be wheeled into the operation room or intensive care treatment unit and become an object of great concern and great financial investment. The patient slowly but surely is beginning to be treated like a thing.

It must be further specified that the aim of medicine is to preserve human health and to cure illness in human beings, not to prolong patient life forever at any cost. Technological advantages in life-support devices raise the issue of quality of life. Should individuals be kept alive in undignified and hopeless states? Do people have the right to die? As for when death occurs, except sudden death, a prime issue is when a person should be permitted to die, or whether that should never happen. There is no clear consensus among older people about whether "heroic" measures should be used to keep them alive or whether death should be speeded in hopeless cases involving great pain. The right-to-die movement has grown in recent years and has given rise to new discussions of voluntary euthanasia, or elective death.

Distinctions are made between two types of euthanasia: active (causing death) and passive (allowing death). Active euthanasia (commission) occurs when death is induced by a deliberate attempt to end a person's life, such as the injection of a lethal dose of a drug. Passive euthanasia (omission) occurs when a person is allowed to die by withholding an available treatment, such as withdrawing a life-sustaining therapeutic device. Today, active euthanasia is illegal in all countries of the world except the Netherlands, but the trend is toward acceptance of passive euthanasia in the case of terminally ill patients. Among those with long dying trajectories, age is an important element in determining what is expected of them.

Young people are expected to fight death and to try to finish business in their remaining time. Older people who are dying are expected to show more passive acceptance.

With specific regard to euthanasia, the following questions may be asked: What is an individual dying of a terminal disease obliged to do? What is he permitted to do? What is a physician treating a terminal patient obliged to do? What is he permitted to do? When is it right to die? It is not our right to keep the patient alive and suffering but our obligation to reduce the patient's affliction. The terminal patient ought to be given at least the same consideration as a criminal about to be executed for committing a capital offense. We have the obligation to reduce the criminals' affliction when they are dying; we treat the criminal with mercy.

In Holland, an estimated 90,000 citizens carry "euthanasia passports," which request assistance with self-initiated suicide if certain medical conditions arise; approximately 4,000 physician-assisted suicides occur each year.[19] In the United States, the Supreme Court has ruled that physician-assisted suicide for terminally ill patients is not a constitutional right. Consequently, there are likely to be test cases at the court.

The October 24, 2003, *News & Observer* reported that a Florida resident, Mrs. Terri Schiavo, had been in what doctors call a "persistent vegetative state" since 1990. Her husband, Michael Schiavo, was involved in one of the nation's longest and most contentious right-to-die legal battles. He asked that all the feeding tubes be removed, which they were by a court order on October 15, but the legislature of Florida passed a bill designed to keep Terri Schiavo alive. The Florida governor invoked the law and ordered the feeding tube reinserted.

It can be argued that these legal actions were conducted with political motivation. The legal costs of this case since 1990 were mostly supported by tax money. This case was an ideological war to determine whose value and interest was dominant. In other words, it was an ideological war between the doctrine of sanctity of life and the doctrine of quality of life.

The doctrine of sanctity of life is opposed by the doctrine of quality of life. The quality of life principle states that the value a life contains is more important than mere living. The sanctity of life view sees even the worst human existence as positive. Not to live is tragic, and the more life there is, the better. The quality of life view regards some lives as having positive value and others as having negative value. A man who retires from life does no harm to society; he only ceases to do good.

Even Jesus, usually seen as the paragon of respect for life, said to Judas: "It were better that he were never born" (Matt 26:24), suggesting that nonexistence is preferable to an evil existence. An evil life has negative worth; it is bad. Evil is associated with gratuitous suffering and pain, with doing things harmful to others. Hence, we might conclude that even from a Christian perspective, death is preferable to excruciating pain without the expectation of remission. For the Christian, death, as the end of conscious life, really doesn't exist. Eternal blessedness awaits the faithful, although it is not a soul but a transformed glorified body that inherits heaven.[20]

In the changing field of medicine, we have to ask ourselves whether medicine is to remain a humanitarian and respected profession or a new but depersonalized science in the service of prolonging life rather than diminishing human suffering. Since the adoption of the Hippocratic oath, the physician no longer has absolute freedom of action, even in seeking to advance medical science. None dares attribute any other aim to medicine than the one Hippocrates (460–377 BC) assigned it. At this point it seems fitting to quote from that famous oath:[21]

> The regiment I adopt shall be for the benefit of my patients according to my ability and judgment, and not for their hurt or for any wrong. I will give no deadly drug to any, though it be asked of me, nor will I counsel such ... Whatsoever house I enter, there will I go for the benefit of the sick, refraining from all wrongdoing or corruption, and especially from any act of seduction ...

Often the attempt to prolong life merely prolongs a hospitalized death. Few Americans want to end their lives that way. Without a living will, doctors will continue to follow the Hippocratic oath and to perform costly and painful procedures on patients who do not (or would not) want them, and who will die in a few days or weeks anyway.

Most people would likely agree that it is not humane to prolong the life of a patient who is living in a coma with no hope of recovery. But the threat of lawsuits has often caused doctors and hospitals to connect such patients with life-preserving intensive-care equipment. Once this has been done, medical personnel are understandably cautious about removing this equipment, even in cases that appear utterly hopeless.

According to James Rachels, the euthanasia issue ultimately comes down to a question of morality. In a discussion of the concept of the individual's welfare, he argues that we should cease speaking about maximizing "happiness," the traditional moralist's approach, and shift instead to speaking about maximizing "interests." This leads to a more utilitarian conception that results in the following justification of euthanasia:[22]

- If an action promotes the best interests of everyone concerned, then the action is morally acceptable.

- In at least some cases, euthanasia promotes the best interests of everyone concerned.

- Therefore, in at least some cases euthanasia is morally acceptable.

Rachels also lists five features when we think of euthanasia.[23] This is generally adopted as a guideline of reference.

1. The patient is suffering from an irreversible, terminal illness.

2. The illness has reduced the patient to a condition that, for him, is intolerable.

3. While of sound mind, the patient asks to be killed, and the request is repeated over a substantial period of time.

4. The killing is motivated to end the patient's suffering and provide him with a "good death."

5. The patient is killed in response to his own request.

We should not play God; our culture traditionally has recognized that only God gives life and only God should take life away. It can be argued that the intervention of modern medicine, such as life-sustaining apparatus, to keep people alive that otherwise would have long since died might itself be interfering with God's plan. I believe that God didn't intend for his creatures to live forever. What could be more like "playing God" than keeping people alive artificially?[24]

The politics of health considers health care to be one of the benefits of society and its associated costs one of the burdens that society must distribute. When terminally ill patients ask for euthanasia voluntarily, society should respect and honor their decision, which also reduces the burden on society. Instead, the law prohibits it. This is illogical and very strange to me.

In summary, I would say that the arguments on euthanasia are a typical example of economic conflict and ideological war. The business of the pharmaceutical industry, hospitals, and the whole health care system is to make money. Euthanasia is bad for business. Furthermore, the expansion of bureaucracy of the health system, population growth, and patients' unrealistic demand for a long life—all the objective reality and subjective reality combined together—pushes the argument on euthanasia beyond control.

Argument on Euthanasia from the Religious Perspective

In most societies, death is not viewed as the end of existence—though the biological body has died, the spiritual body is believed to live on. Christians have used of the Sixth Commandment, "Thou shalt not kill," as the basis for the prohibition of suicide since St. Augustine (AD 354–430). Yet the term "kill"in the Sixth Commandment actually means "wrong killing." The Sixth Commandment thus does not serve as a general prohibition of self-killing, since self-killing may not always be wrongful killing. Therefore, in the Revised Version of the English Bible (1885), the commandment reads, "Thou shalt do no murder."

In early Christianity, suicide was sometimes regarded as a virtuous act. In the fourth century, recognizing that certain Christian women had committed suicide rather than permit their bodies to be ravaged, Bishop Augustine granted that they may have done what was right in the sight of God. In the thirteenth century, St. Thomas Aquinas, the most outstanding of Catholic theologians, gave three succinct arguments as to why suicide is a sin:[25]

1. Suicide is contrary to nature; every living organism naturally desires to preserve its life.

2. It is contrary to our social obligations: the whole human community is injured by self-killing.

3. Suicide is contrary to our religious rights: God alone should decide when a person will live or die.

If euthanasia is not acceptable to some religious people, then by the same logic they should not ask for organ transplants. God created us with only one organ for each function in our body to sustain life. The human body is a holy work of God's creation. Our body was not created as a living organ warehouse. Changing anything in our body or moving anything from our body is a violation of God's creation. Would you change a brushstroke on a painting by Picasso? If our organ works well, it is a blessing; if it does not work well, let be it without any alteration. The human body is much more holy than Picasso's art. Euthanasia and organ transplant are the two sides of the same coin. If we are against one; we should not accept the other. We cannot conduct our life according to our own convenience without any principle.

If "playing God" simply means doing what will influence our chances of living or dying, a lot of responsible social actions do that. If, on the other hand, it means unwarrantedly affecting the life chances of someone, the question when dealing with the dying process boils down to what is morally correct behavior.

David Hume (1711–1776) made the simple but devastating point that if it is for God alone to decide when we shall live and when we shall die, then "it would be equally criminal to act for the preservation of life as for its destruction. It is a kind of blasphemy to imagine that any created being can disturb the order of the world, or invade the business of Providence. Hume put the point this way in his work *On Suicide*, in 1784: "If I turn aside a stone which is falling upon my head, I disturbed the course of nature; and I invade the peculiar province of the Almighty, by lengthening my life beyond the period, which, by the general laws of matter and motion, He has assigned it."[26]

In summary, I would emphasize three features: First, changing the state of our bodies is a transgression of our duty to God, including improvement. Second, if we accept the Bible as the absolute, unequivocal words of God, we must accept them all; "selective enforcement" as we please is immoral. Third, it is not our role to judge; it is God's. "Judge not lest you be judged" (Matthew 7:1). Unfortunately, the self-interest of bureaucracy of the health system and the patient's unrealistic demand for a long life combined together pushes the argument on euthanasia beyond control.

Argument on Euthanasia from Sociological Perspective

Debate over euthanasia has a long history. In the first century AD, the Roman philosopher Seneca stated, "If I can choose between a death of torture and one that is simple and easy, why should I not select the latter? Why should I endure the agonies of disease? When I can emancipate myself from all my torture? I will not depart by death from disease as long as it may be healed and leaves my mind unimpaired, but if I know that I will suffer forever, I will depart, not through fear of pain itself, but because it prevents all for which I live."[27] As you can see, the argument over euthanasia has been going on for two thousand years. There are essentially three arguments in favor of active euthanasia:

1. **The right to life includes the right to die.** If I have a right to live as I see fit, then so long as I am not harming others I can do what I like with my life, including waive that right and put myself to death.

2. **The Golden Rule argument.** The Golden Rule states that we should do unto others as we would have others do unto us (if we were in their

shoes). The Golden Rule seems to advise us to help people who are being tortured by pain and who have no hope of remission to do what they would like to do.

3. **The combined argument from the standpoint of freedom and the prevention of cruelty.** Two of the basic values of a civilized society are freedom and the elimination of cruelty or unnecessary suffering. Freedom dictates that we allow terminally ill patients to choose whether they want to die sooner and without pain, and the principle of preventing cruelty dictates that we do whatever is necessary to help them die.

Patients should be allowed to make life-and-death decisions, because who is more likely to be totally and lovingly concerned with patients' best interests than the patient himself? We must recognize that a person's right to decide to live or die overrides anyone else's right to decide for that person. There are essentially four arguments against voluntary active euthanasia. I will list them here, as well as my rebuttal of each:[28]

1. The oldest is the argument from natural law. They argue that we have a natural inclination to preserve life and that active euthanasia violates natural law. Yet, if we follow only the natural course of things, then we should not build a dam to divert a river from its natural course to prevent the flooding of a city, and medicine itself would be prohibited.

2. The second argument is that voluntary active euthanasia is "playing God" and violates the sanctity of life. Yet the term "playing God" is just a pejorative way of emoting against autonomous action. If playing God simply means doing what will affect the chances of living or dying, a lot of responsible social actions do that. If playing God means affecting the prospects of death, then using medicine to keep a sick person from dying is playing God,. To employ antibiotics to kill harmful bacteria may be playing God. We are stewards of God's property, so we may not mishandle it or throw it away by killing it. Of course, we are also responsible for using our reason in handling God's property. We do take lives in self-defense, so why not act in self-defense against torture or great and irreversible suffering? The best way to exercise stewardship towards God's property is to use the best reasoning available in deciding how to use that property.

3. The third argument is that allowing voluntary active euthanasia may lead to abuses of the law. Yet the fact that a practice can be abused does

not mean that it shouldn't be used at all. Salt and sugar can be abused and harm us, but that doesn't mean that they shouldn't be used at all. Knives, cars, and drugs can be abused, but that doesn't mean that they should be outlawed.

4. Finally, those opposed to active euthanasia appeal to the difference between killing and letting die. Yet while passive euthanasia may sometimes be justified, it doesn't follow that active euthanasia is. What is the difference between killing and letting die? What counts are our motives and the deliberation that goes into our acts.

Some opponents of legalized voluntary euthanasia argue that we can never be sure that a request to be killed is the result of a free and rational decision. Might not the sick and elderly be pressured by their relatives to end their lives quickly? Will it not be possible to commit outright murder by pretending that a person has requested euthanasia? And even if there is no pressure or falsification, can anyone who is ill, suffering pain, and very probably in a drugged and confused state of mind make a rational decision about whether to live or die? These questions raise technical difficulties for the legalization of voluntary euthanasia. Voluntary euthanasia societies in Britain and elsewhere have sought to address these difficulties by proposing that euthanasia should be legal only for a person[29]

- who is diagnosed by two doctors as suffering from an incurable illness expected to cause severe distress or the loss of rational faculties;

- who has, at least 30 days before the proposed act of euthanasia, and in the presence of two independent witnesses, made a written request for euthanasia in the event of the situation described in [the point above] occurring.

Only a doctor could administer euthanasia, and if the patient was at the time still capable of consenting, the doctor would have to make sure that the patient still wished the declaration to be acted upon. The patient's declaration could be revoked at any time.

A fundamental principle in both moral and political life in civilized countries is that competent adults possess the right to make personal decisions. As John Stuart Mill argued in *On Liberty*,

> That principle is, that the sole end for which mankind are warranted, individually or collectively in interfering with the liberty of action of any of their members, is self-protection. That the only purpose for which power can be

rightfully exercised over any member of a civilized community, against his will, is to prevent harm to others ... Over himself, over his body and mind, the individual is sovereign ... The only freedom which desires the name, is that of pursuing our own good in our own way, so long as we do not attempt to deprive others of theirs, or impede their effort to obtain it.

For Mill, the individual freedoms that rightfully belong to us are the ones that will maximize human happiness. He felt very strongly that the only freedom that will not maximize human happiness is the freedom to harm others. Euthanasia does not harm others.

The principle of respect for autonomy tells us to allow rational agents to live their own lives according to their own autonomous decisions, free from coercion or interference; but if rational agents should autonomously choose to die, then respect for autonomy will lead us to assist them to do as they choose.

There are two general classes of interferences that Mill's principle would prohibit. First, we cannot force a person to conform to our ideas of right and wrong so long as the person is not harming others. For example, we have no business trying to force people to stop being homosexuals. Second, if Mill's principle is correct, then we may not interfere with a person's action "for his own good." For example, if someone is feeling poorly, we may advise or urge a visit to a doctor, but we have no right to force this on a person, even "for his own good."

The relevant question is this: Does the conduct of someone who chooses to die affect anyone other than him or herself, the "consenting adult" who is involved in the affair? If not, then others have no right to interfere. If humanity depends on social recognition, individuals or whole groups may be dehumanized by being denied any status in their society. An act of euthanasia, in which the patient requests a lethal drug and the doctor provides it, is a "private affair" in this sense; those participating are "consenting adults," and no one else's interests need be involved. Therefore, we should respect the rights of dying patients.

Two arguments might be given to show that euthanasia is a justified exception to the ethical rule against killing.[30] First, killing is objectionable only because, in normal cases, the person who is killed loses something of great value—life itself. In being deprived of life, a person is harmed. In euthanasia, however, this is not true. If a dying person whose life holds nothing but torment says that such a life no longer has value, the claim surely can be deemed a reasonable judgment. Second, killing a person is usually a violation of the individual's right to life. But if a person asks to be killed, the killing is not a violation of individual rights. (This is a general point that applies to other rights as well. If, for example, you steal something that belongs to me, you violate my property rights, but if I ask you to take it and you do, then you do not violate my rights.) For these reasons, saying that euthanasia is a violation of the rule against killing is not enough to prove that it is wrong.

Finally, it must be admitted that if active euthanasia were legalized, there would inevitably be some abuses, just as there are abuses of virtually every social practice. No one can deny it. The crucial issue is whether the abuses or the bad consequences generally, would be so numerous as to outweigh the advantages of legalized euthanasia. The possibility of bad consequences should make us proceed cautiously in this area, but it should not stop us from proceeding at all.[30] A famous Chinese proverb says, "We should not give up eating for fear of choking," which means that we should not refrain from doing something necessary for fear of a slight risk.

Viewpoints on Death from Different Cultural Perspectives

The ancient Greeks faced death as they faced life—openly and directly. To live a full life and die with glory was the prevailing goal of the Greeks. In most societies, death is not viewed as the end of existence—though the biological body has died, the spiritual body is believed to live on. This religious perspective is favored by Americans as well. However, cultures differ in their perceptions of death and their reactions to it. For example, some cultures' attitudes toward death include beliefs about reincarnation, which is an important aspect of the Hindu and Buddhist religions.

Perceptions of death reflect diverse values and philosophies. Death may be seen as a punishment for one's sins, an act of atonement, or a judgment of a just God. For some, death means loneliness; for others, death is a quest for happiness. For still others, death represents redemption; or a relief from the trials and tribulations of the earthly world. Some embrace death and welcome it; others abhor and fear it. For those who welcome it, death may be seen as the fitting end of a fulfilled life. These perspectives serve to illustrate that how we depart from Earth is influenced by how we have lived.

What happens to man in a society bent on ignoring or avoiding death? What factors, if any, contribute to an increasing anxiety in relation to death? In many ways, we are "death avoiders" and "death deniers" in the United States. This is clearly a hypocritical attitude for most Americans: For people who believe that there is life after death with God in heaven, isn't it a glory to be with God finally? But they abhor and fear death. Maybe they fear they won't be going to heaven but rather to the other place. This would certainly make death fearful for many. This denial can take many forms:[31]

- The tendency of the funeral industry to gloss over death and fashion life-like qualities in the dead

- The adoption of euphemistic language for death—for example, "exiting" or "passing on" instead of "dying"

- The persistent search for a fountain of youth

- The rejection and isolation of the aged, who may remind us of death

- The adoption of the concept of pleasant and rewarding afterlife, suggesting that we are immortal

- The medical community's emphasis on prolonging biological life rather than diminishing human suffering

Even though we are death avoiders and deniers, ultimately we face death. Death is not an option; death always occurs after birth takes place. It is not a possibility but a certainty. It is a well-known fact that some animals have a kind of presentment about their death. When they "realize" that their end is eminent, they lay themselves down and await their end.

Many of our contemporary attitudes toward dying and funeral practices after death seek to negate the naturalness of this element in the life cycle. On the other hand, Jewish tradition confronts death directly, regarding the period of terminal illness and dying as a time when loved ones should surround, comfort, and encourage the patient. According to the Halacha (the Jewish legal system), "If there is some exterior force preventing the expiration of life (lit. the exit of the soul from the body) it is permitted to remove it."[32] Rabbi Immanuel Jakobovis suggests in his study *Jewish Medical Ethics* that "Jewish law sanctions, and perhaps even demands, the withdrawal of any factor—whether extraneous to the patient himself or not—which may artificially delay his demise on the final phase. It might be argued that this modification implies the legality of expediting the death of an incurable patient in acute agony by withholding from him such medicaments as sustains his continued life by unnatural means—an issue also considered in Catholic moral philosophy."[32]

When the family and community face the prospect of the death of one of its members, Jewish law reminds us that "a dying man is considered the same as a living man in every respect." Americans treat the dying differently than we do the living. The dying person lives alone in an artificial environment, created by those who do not wish to cope with the fact of death. Halacha forbids this dishonest approach. Further, the Jewish tradition of never leaving the bedside of the dying is of immense value, not only to the dying person but also to those about to be bereaved. How helpless and how guilty we must feel when we hear of the death of a loved one, especially if no one was there to ease the fear of uncertainty and the pain of separation.[32] A funeral according to Halacha emphasizes that death is death; realism and simplicity are characteristics of the Jewish burial. In this respect, it stands in clear contrast to the American funeral ritual.

Believing in resurrection of the body, Muslims bury their dead reverently and quickly, treating the bodies with care and respect. When death occurs, the body is washed and shrouded and buried as soon as possible, preferably within a day. Though the service for the dead is standard, with minor variations according to the practice of various schools, burial customs vary. In Saudi Arabia, the body of the deceased is laid in a shallow grave scooped out of the desert. In Egypt, the body is sealed in a coffin and entombed in a mausoleum. The tombs of some wealthy Egyptians are among Cairo's most prominent architectural landmarks.[33] The most famous ones are the royal tombs—the Pyramids at Giza.

In the East, the Buddhist concept of reincarnation is different from Christian thinking. Buddhism stresses that life and death make up an eternal wheel, called "wheel of life." Each individual is attached to the wheel, and attached to each individual is karma. Any act or intention harmful to you and others is karma, which can affect us in next life. People supposedly purge their karmas by successive incarnations. The Buddha did not hold that the "reborn" being is the same as the being who died. Thus, strictly speaking, this is not a case of rebirth. The reborn being is linked to the being who died by a causal process (karmic causality). Thus, at death these factors in complex ways enter into the causal process (karmic causality), which leads to another embodied individual occurring in direct dependence upon actions performed by former being. Karmic causation is central to holding the whole process together. Depending on how we live this life, we will be reincarnated in a future earthly existence into a bodily form fitting our moral worth in this life. People who live nobly will be born with added talents and opportunities.[34] Many Buddhists seek not heaven but permanent liberation from the cyclical round of birth, death, and rebirth, which means never returning to the "wheel of life." It is an eternal emancipation.

In Chinese culture, the goal of life is the establishment, maintenance, and enjoyment of harmony in this world. Harmony is enhanced if the individual is submerged in the group. This means that this world, not the other-worldly heaven, has the potential to fulfill the deepest needs and highest ideals of human life. It also means that orderliness is vital to the good life: all things, natural as well as human, must have a proper place and function within the whole. The ancient Chinese felt that the survival of human life depended on harmony and order. The Chinese neither held out the promise of heavenly bliss nor feared hellish punishment but rather sought a this-worldly salvation.[35]

When Confucius was asked about death, he replied, "Why do you ask me about death when you do not know how to live?"[36] Regarding the concept of a deity, Confucius was an agnostic. Nevertheless, he did not oppose the traditional view, and throughout its history, Confucianism has stressed heavily the cult of ancestors. Confucius turned men's thoughts not to the future but to the past, to the way of the ancestors.

Confucius emphasized that a person should focus his attention on living a good life. The afterlife, with its rewards or punishments, is not within one's control and thus should not be the point of emphasis.[37] The important thing is to live a virtuous life first. In addition, the doctrine of karma and reincarnation added a new dimension to the way the Chinese thought about ancestors and the afterlife. It became a part of the theory of ancestor worship.

My Personal Experience and Feelings

I am eighty years old now. I have the experience of aging but not dying and death. Judging by my health, I don't think I will experience dying and death in the near future. I am sorry you have to wait for a while to hear my dying experience; however, I am able to tell you what I feel about dying but not death. Death itself is mute, and it renders us speechless … As long as we are alive, we cannot expect death itself to provide the answer on the question of death.

I know one thing for sure: Death always has been and always will be with us; it is an integral part of human existence, and it can occur only after birth takes place. As Benjamin Franklin said in 1789, "In this world nothing can be said to be certain except death and taxes."

If I am dying of a terminal disease and suffering, my right to decide to live or die should override anyone else's right to decide for me. The right to live and to die is innate, and it does not need social recognition as long as I don't harm others. If there are any moral rights at all, there is at least one prior right founded on justice—the equal right of all persons to be free to decide to live or die. As John Stuart Mill argued famously, "The only freedom which desires the name, is that of pursuing our own good in our own way, so long as we do not attempt to deprive others of theirs, or impede their effort to obtain it." Voluntary euthanasia does not harm others. It seems to me that it is only a matter of time until laws will passed that permit the administration of voluntary euthanasia when the only alternative is an agonizing or meaningless existence. I sincerely hope they become a reality in my lifetime.

The argument for beneficent euthanasia is twofold. First, it is not only virtuous to help most where help is most needed, but it is often a duty to do so. Second, in addition to the argument of kindness, there is an argument of justice. Justice requires that where possible we give to each according to need; and since human beings have a basic need to live and die with dignity, it is just that we treat them accordingly.[38] The patient has the right to say yes or no to alternatives. We live in a democratic society; unfortunately, decisions about our lives are often made by others, and the elderly are made to feel powerless.

I am mortal, but death never scares me. In my life, I merely raised a family with two good children. I haven't made any contribution to mankind, and I don't think I am qualified to go to heaven. If the ashes of my body can be used as fertilizer for an oak tree, it would be a great honor to me! Dying is the one thing no one can do for me; I must die alone. Finally I would like to quote Reinhold Niebuhr's well-known prayer[39] for all of us to think about:

Lord, give me the courage to change the things which can be changed.
And give me the patience to accept the things that cannot be changed.
But most of all, give me the wisdom to know the difference.

Wisdom lies in living a life in which we know when to exercise courage and when to exercise resignation. Death is a case that calls for both. We resign ourselves to the unalterable fact that we will die, but we courageously overcome any useless perturbations over that fact.

Notes

1. Eberhard Jungel, *Death: The Riddle and The Mystery* (Philadelphia: The Westminster Press, 1974), vii, 9–11, 121–36.

2. Carol K. Sigelman and David R. Shaffer, *Life-span Human Development*, 2nd ed. (Pacific Grove, CA, Brooks/Cole Publishing Company, 1995), 480–81.

3. Fredric D. Wolinsky, *The Sociology of Health* (Belmont, CA: Wadsworth Publishing Company, 1988), 181.

4. Nancy R. Hooyman and H. Asuman Kiyak, *Social Gerontology*, 3rd ed. (Boston: Allyn and Bacon, 1993), 388.

5. B. Downing, ed., *Euthanasia and the Right to Death* (Los Angeles: Nash Publishing, 1969), 19.

6. Thomas Nagel, *Mortal Questions* (New York: Cambridge University Press, 1979), 1–3.

7. Elisabeth Kubler-Ross, *Death: The Final Stage of Growth* (Englewood Cliffs, NJ: Prentice-Hall, Inc., 1975), 160.

8. Joseph Fletcher, *Humanhood: Essays in Biomedical Ethics* (New York: Prometheus Books, 1979), 150–54.

9. B. Downing, ed., *Euthanasia and the Right to Death* (Los Angeles: Nash Publishing, 1969), 14–16.

10. William H. Shaw, *Social and Personal Ethics*, 3rd ed., (New York: Wadsworth Publishing Company, 1999), 7–8.

11. John Stuart Mill, *Utilitarianism* (New York: The\Bobbs-Merrill Company, Inc., 1957), 10.

12. Louis P. Pojman, *Life and Death: Grappling with the Moral Dilemma of Our Time,* 2nd ed. (New York: Wadswouth Publishing Company, 2000), 37, 38, 40.

13. Tom Regan, ed., *Matters of Life and Death* (New York: McGraw-Hill, Inc., 1993), 49.

14. H. J. Paton, *Immanuel Kant Groundwork of the Metaphysic of Morals* (New York: Harper & Row Publishers, 1953), 30–32.

15. William H. Shaw, *Social & Personal Ethics*, 3rd ed., (New York: Wadsworth Publishing Company, 1999), 23–27.

16. Pojman, *Life and Death*, 51.

17. Shaw, *Social and Personal Ethics*, 45, 46, 69.

18. M. Velasquez and C. Rostankowski, *Ethics Theory and Practice* (Englewood Cliffs, NJ: Practice-Hall, Inc., 1985), 302, 304.

19. Barry D. Pherson, *Aging as a Social Process* (Tononto, Canada: Harcourt Brace & Company, 1998), 364.

20. Pojman, *Life and Death,* 60–68.

21. R. L. Bruckberger, *Image of America* (New York: The Viking Press, 1959), 137.

22. Wolinsky, *Sociology of Health*, 190.

23. Regan, *Life and Death*, 3.

24. Jeffrey Olen and Vincent Barry, *Applying Ethics* (Belmont, CA: Wadworth Publishing Company, 1989), 202.

25. P. T. Jersild and D. A. Johnson, *Moral Issues and Christian Response*, 4th ed. (Chicago: Holt, Rinehart, and Winston, Inc., 1988), 397.

26. Regan, *Life and Death*, 53.

27. Russell A. Ward, *The Aging Experience: An Introduction to Social Gerontology* (New York: J. B. Lippincott Company, 1979), 484.

28. Pojman, *Life and Death,* 89–92.

29. Peter Singer, *Practical Ethics* (New York: Cambridge University Press, 1979), 142–44.

30. Regan, *Life and Death*, 51, 54–55, 63.

31. John W. Santrock, *Life-span Development* (Dubuque, IA: Wm. C. Brown Publishers, 1992), 634–37.

32. Kubler-Ross, *Death*, 38–42, 44–45, 46–47.

33. Thomas W. Lippman, *Understanding Islam* (New York: Penguin Group, 1990), 17.

34. Paul Williams, *Buddhist Thought* (New York: Routledge, 2000), 56, 69.

35. Niels C. Nielsen Jr. et al., *Religions of the World*, 3rd ed. (New York: St. Martin's Press, 1993), 224.

36. David G. Bradley, *A Guide to the World's Religions* (Englewood Cliffs, NJ: Prentice-Hall, Inc., 1963), 147.

37. Lian Chew and Phyllis Ghim, *The Chinese Religion and the Baha'i Faith* (Oxford: George Ronald, 1993), 32, 180.

38. Marvin Kohl, *Beneficent Euthanasia* (New York: Prometheus Books, 1975), 135.

39. Pojman, *Life and Death*, 69.

8

Looking Ahead

Looking Ahead

Looking ahead is related to one's overall aim in life, which is a value judgment. No matter if one is young or old, as long as we are living beings, we have to retain interest in things and have hope for tomorrow—looking ahead at what is worthwhile in a human life enables us to find acceptance of conditions beyond our control (e.g. aging, death). One's overall aim in life depends on one's value judgment and perspective. Generally speaking, one can specify one's overall aim in life in three ways:[1]

1. What one can have or possess

2. What one can do or accomplish

3. What one can be

In old age, it is useless to possess too many material things, and it is too late to accomplish big projects; only the third of these three is the most realistic way of specifying one's overall aims. Most elderly look ahead for a healthy, happy, and serene life, but aging and death are always a shadow in their minds without a satisfactory solution.

Dr. Robert Butler, former director of the National Institute on Aging, observes that it is easier to manage the problem of death than the problem of living as an old person. Aging is the gradual fulfillment of the life cycle; aging does not need to be hidden or denied, but it can be understood, affirmed, and experienced as a process of growth given by God. An anonymous poet has described the aging process very well:[2]

Age is a quality of mind.
If you have left your dreams behind,
If hope is cold,

If you no longer look ahead,
If your ambition's fires are dead—
Then you are old (and dead in life).
But if from life you take the best.
And if in life you keep the zest,
If love you hold—
No matter how the years go by,
No matter how the birthdays fly,
You are not old (but alive)!

Death is the final stage of growth in this life. The self or spirit, or whatever you may wish to label it, is eternal. As Kubler-Ross said, "Death may be viewed as the curtain between the existence that we are conscious of and one that is hidden from us until we raise that curtain."[3] There is no need to be afraid of death. It is the denial of death that is partially responsible for people living empty and purposeless lives. In contrast, when you fully understand that each day you awaken could be the last you have, you take the time that day to grow, to become more of who you really are, to reach out to other human beings. It is imperative that each of you, no matter how many days or weeks or months or years you have to live, commit yourself to growth.[3]

We must learn to die in order that we may learn to live; growing to be who you truly are requires sometimes that you die to the life chosen for you by society; each new step of growth involves throwing off more of the shackles restraining you. Spiritually speaking, in order to grow, you must continuously die and be reborn, much as a caterpillar becomes a butterfly.[4] Ann Landers wrote a poem "Why Worry" about our feeling of death, which is funny and encouraging:[5]

There are only two things to worry about—
Either you are well, or you are sick.
If you are well, then there is nothing to worry about.
But if you are sick, there are two things to worry about—
Either you will get well, or you will die.
If you get well, then there is nothing to worry about.
But if you die, there are only two things to worry about.
Either you go to heaven or to hell.
If you go to heaven, there is nothing to worry about.
If you go to hell, you'll be so busy shaking hands with old friends,
You won't have time to worry.

Five hundred years BC, when Confucius was asked about death, he replied, "Why do you ask me about death when you do not know how to live?" As Confucius himself put it, "Devote yourself earnestly to the duties due to men, and respect spiritual beings, but keep them at a distance" (Analects 6.20). The distancing of spiritual beings was both a sign of respect for their power and a refocusing of religious concerns onto human affairs. Confucius tells us to pay attention to this world and not to worry about the other world.[6] If you are not used to Confucius' thinking, Archibald MacLeish wrote a short poem[7] which is similar to what Confucius said in meaning but with more philosophical flavor:

> We have learned the answers, all the answers:
> It is the question that we do not know.

The majority of people worry that they don't have the perfect answer. Maybe we worry for nothing. If we don't know the question, why should we worry for answer? Let us enjoy our life now.

My Personal Experience and Feelings

When I was young, I looked forward to be an adult. When I was an adult, I looked forward to becoming an engineer—and I did. When I was in my sixties, I looked forward to retiring, and then I could do what I would like to do. After retiring, I did consulting work to help one American company establish a joint venture with China in the 1990s. But I was not happy working in the industrial field anymore and also tired of traveling across Pacific Ocean so often, so in 1996 I completely retired from working and registered at North Carolina State University (NCSU) as a full-time student majoring in philosophy. My goal is to find the meaning of life before it is too late.

It is recognized that continued learning and problem solving in later life can sustain and even improve intellectual abilities, attitudes, and interests. The stimulation provided by an educational atmosphere is an enriching experience for many elderly people, and thereby important to their physical and mental health.

Because of my age and because I'm afraid of driving, I moved to a house only two blocks away from NCSU. I can walk to school in old age as long as I can walk. In these ten years of studying, I have gradually come to understand that what is worthwhile in a human life enables us to accept conditions beyond our control (e.g., aging, death). One's overall aim in life depends not on what one can have or possess, not what one can do or accomplish, but on what one can be.

I fully agree with what Confucius said: "Why do you ask me about death when you do not know how to live?" I have no fear about aging and death, no fear at all, and I don't even have time to think about it. As long as I am not senile, I will keep studying and searching for the truth—what is the overall aim of life?

Finally, I'd like to share two famous sayings with all my fellow senior citizens: (1) "People don't grow old. When they stop growing, they become old." And (2) "Death is not the greatest loss in life. The greatest loss is what dies inside us while we live."[8]

Notes

1. William H. Shaw, *Social and Personal Ethics*, 3rd ed. (New York: Wadsworth Publishing Company, 1999), 69.

2. Gari Lesnoff-Caravaglia, *Values, Ethics, and Aging* (New York: Human Sciences Press, Inc., 1985), 26, 153.

3. Elisabeth Kubler-Ross, *Death: The Final Stage of Growth* (Englewood Cliffs, NJ: Prentice-Hall, Inc., 1975), 166.

4. Ibid., 147.

5. Ann Landers, *Why Worry* (Chicago: Creators Syndicate).

6. Niels C. Nielsen Jr. et al., *Religions of The World*, 3rd ed. (New York: St. Martin's Press, 1993), 224, 230.

7. Alvin Toffler, ed., *The Futurists* (New York: Random House, 1972), 48.

8. John Robbins, *Healthy at 100* (New York: Random House, 2006), 3, 191.

Index

Note: page entries followed by an "f" and "t" indicate that the reference is to a figure and table, respectively.

978-0-595-43692-
0-595-43692-7

www.ingramcontent.com/pod-product-compliance
Lightning Source LLC
Chambersburg PA
CBHW021544290526
45785CB00004BA/1514